PERFECT PHRASES
in Spanish

for

CONSTRUCTION

PERFECT PHRASES
in Spanish
for
CONSTRUCTION

**500+ Essential Words and Phrases
for Communicating with Spanish-Speakers**

Jean Yates

New York Chicago San Francisco Lisbon London Madrid Mexico City
Milan New Delhi San Juan Seoul Singapore Sydney Toronto

The **McGraw·Hill** Companies

Library of Congress Cataloging-in-Publication Data

Yates, Jean.
    Perfect phrases in Spanish for construction : 500+ essential words and phrases
for communicating with Spanish-speakers / Jean Yates.
        p.   cm. — (Perfect phrases in Spanish)
    ISBN 0-07-149475-8 (alk. paper)
    1. Spanish language—Conversation and phrase books (for construction industry
employees).   I. Title.

    PC4120.C64Y38   2008
    468.3'421024624—dc22   2008004597

1 2 3 4 5 6 7 8 9 10 11 12 13 14 15 16 17 18 19 20 21   DOC/DOC   0 9 8

ISBN 978-0-07-149475-5
MHID   0-07-149475-8

McGraw-Hill books are available at special quantity discounts to use as premiums and
sales promotions or for use in corporate training programs. To contact a representative,
please visit the Contact Us pages at www.mhprofessional.com.

This book is printed on acid-free paper.

The author would like to thank Leonard Leshuk for his on-all-hands knowledge and advice, and Luis Coronel, Chad Yates, Jack Clark, Karen Young, and Nancy Hall for their suggestions, advice, and support.

Contents

Contents

Contents

CHAPTER 5 INDOOR CONSTRUCTION WORK   91

Contents

Introduction

I n many parts of the United States, individuals and companies are increasingly employing Spanish-speaking painters, plumbers, electrical workers, carpenters, and other general workers in the construction industry who do not speak English. This book is designed to provide such employers with simple phrases in Spanish that will enable them to communicate basic information to their employees, helping to ensure that they understand the information necessary for jobs to be done correctly, efficiently, and safely.

It is very common for people who do not speak each other's language to communicate with hand signals, gestures, or words they may have heard others say. This may lead to a certain level of mutual understanding, but it is less than ideal, especially in a job setting, as it often ends in misunderstandings by both parties. It can cause mishaps and bad feelings, and, especially in the construction industry, it can be dangerous. In this book, employers will find key words and phrases that will help them to communicate with their Spanish-speaking workers clearly and correctly right from the beginning. Although this is not a course in grammar or conversation, those who consistently use these words and phrases with their employees will find that they are beginning to understand and use quite a bit of Spanish, and they can build on this foundation to continue learning the language.

How This Book Is Organized

The phrases in this book are divided into five chapters. In Chapter 1, you will find general words and phrases that are used every day for saying hello, good-bye, please, thank you, and for expressing other common courtesies. Also in this chapter are the phrases that will enable you to hire and terminate help and to explain to an employee your general rules and policies of employment, including such topics as wages, Social Security payments, punctuality, and so forth. You will also find the words to help you express satisfaction or dissatisfaction with an employee's performance. In Chapter 2, you will find the phrases that express the policies that you set for your employees. Chapter 3 includes phrases for giving basic instructions that can be used in all areas of construction work. Chapter 4 provides vocabulary and phrases for specific outdoor jobs, and Chapter 5 includes the same for indoor jobs.

The glossary contains all the English words used in the book with their equivalents in Spanish, plus a table giving the Spanish words for the numbers from 0 to a million.

Vocabulary Guidelines

Throughout the book there are phrases that allow for substitutable words. When this occurs, the word that can be replaced with another is <u>underlined</u>. Then one, two, or more words that could easily replace the underlined word are presented. This feature will help you memorize the most useful phrases and generate an unlimited number of practical sentences. Here is an example:

Wear <u>a hard hat</u>.	**Póngase <u>un casco</u>.**
	(POHNG-gah-seh oon KAHS-koh)
protective equipment	**protección personal**
	(proh-tek-S'YOHN pehr-soh-NAHL)
a body harness	**un arnés del cuerpo**
	(oon ahr-NESS del KWEHR-poh)
an (orange) vest	**un chaleco (anaranjado)**
	(oon chah-LEH-koh ah-nah-rahn-HAH-thoh)

Pronunciation Guidelines

Each phrase in this book is printed in Spanish to the right of its equivalent English phrase, with a guide to its pronunciation written directly underneath. The symbols used are an approximation of how the words would sound if they were written in English, as illustrated below.

Vowels

To make a Spanish vowel sound, open your mouth and place your lips in position, and do not move your lips until you make the next sound.

Spanish Spelling	**Approximate Pronunciation**
a	ah
e	eh
i	ee
o	oh
u	oo

Introduction

To make a vowel combination, begin with the first vowel, then move your lips into the position of the second.

ai	eye
ei	ay (like the *ei* in *weight*)
oi	oy
ui	wee
ia	yah
ie	yeh
io	yoh
iu	yoo
au	ah'oo
eu	eh'oo
ua	wah
ue	weh
uo	woh

Consonants

b	b
ca / co / cu	kah / koh / koo
ce / ci	seh / see
d (to begin a word)	d
d (after a vowel)	th (as in *brother*)
f	f
ga / go / gu	gah / goh / goo
ge / gi	heh / hee
h	silent (like the *h* in *honest*)
j	h

la / le / li / lo / lu	lah / leh / lee / loh / loo
al / el / il / ol / ul	adl / edl / eedl / odl / udl
ll	y / j
m	m
n	n
n (before c / g)	ng (like the *ng* in *finger*)
ña / ñe / ñi / ño / ñu	n'yah / n'yeh / n'yee / n'yoh / n'yoo
p	p
que / qui	keh / kee
r (at the beginning)	rrr (trilled)
r (between vowels)	d / tt / dd
bari	body
beri	Betty
biri	beady
ora	oughtta
vuru	voodoo
rr	rrr (trilled)
s	s
t	t
v	b
x	ks
y	y / j
z	s

Syllables

As a general rule, each syllable that is printed in lowercase letters should be pronounced with the same tone and length, and the syllable printed in capital letters should be emphasized, by saying it a little louder and longer than the others. For example, the word **bueno**, which means *good*, is represented as follows:

good **bueno**
(BWEH-noh)

How to Get the Most Out of This Book

There are many ways you can help build your Spanish vocabulary:

- Use the pronunciation guidelines provided, but also listen to your employees and try to copy their pronunciation.
- Customize your phrases by substituting words with other words from the lists provided, as well as with new words you learn from your employees. Words that are underlined can be substituted with words from the alphabetical lists provided in the English-Spanish Glossary.
- Keep a notebook—ask your employees to say or write down problematical words or expressions; then, if you cannot find the word in this book, seek help from a dictionary or a bilingual speaker.
- To learn new words from your employees, begin right away by memorizing the following question:

How do you say _____ in Spanish? **¿Cómo se dice _____ en español?**
(KOH-moh seh DEE-seh _____ en eh-spahn-YOHL)

The words you get as answers to your question can be added to your notebook to help you remember them.

Cultural Guidelines

In most Spanish-speaking countries, there are three ways to say *you*: **tú**, to a person you generally socialize with; **usted**, to any other person, including a person you work for or who works for you; and **ustedes**, to two or more people you are talking to at the same time. The phrases in this book are given in the **usted** form, and instructions are provided for changing these to the plural **ustedes** form. This will ensure that you are speaking to your employees in a respectful manner that will be appreciated. Employees will also respond to you with this form.

Some Hispanic cultures have a more relaxed concept of time than is generally the case in the United States. You will need to make it clear that arriving for work on time and on the agreed-upon day(s) is very important in this country, and that if an emergency arises that causes an employee to be late or unable to work, you expect to be informed right away.

Because family is very important in Hispanic culture, you may want to have some idea about the family situation of your employees. Your workers may be supporting a number of family members both here and back home. Be sure to make clear to those who work for you what your policies are for time off for family emergencies and celebrations, as well as for personal illness. You may also wish to state right from the beginning your feelings about family members accompanying, visiting, or calling your employee while on the job.

PERFECT PHRASES
in Spanish
for
CONSTRUCTION

Chapter 1

Spanish Basics

Greetings

Exchanging pleasantries and greetings with your Spanish-speaking employees is a great way to begin to build a stronger working relationship.

Hello.	**Hola.**
	(OH-lah)
Good morning.	**Buenos días.**
	(BWEH-nohs DEE-ahs)
Good afternoon.	**Buenas tardes.**
	(BWEH-nahs TAHR-dess)
Good evening.	**Buenas noches.**
	(BWEH-nahs NOH-chess)
Good night.	**Buenas noches.**
	(BWEH-nahs NOH-chess)
Good-bye.	**Adiós.**
	(ah-TH'YOHS)
See you later.	**Hasta luego.**
	(AH-stahl WEH-goh)

Have a nice day.	**Que le vaya bien.** (lit.: May all go well for you—to someone who is leaving)
	(keh leh bah-yah B'YEN)

In Spanish, sometimes you need to change your greeting depending on whether you are speaking to a male or a female, as well as when you speak to several people together. In the examples below, you'll see four ways to say "Welcome":

Welcome. (to a male)	**Bienvenido.**
	(b'yen-beh-NEE-thoh)
Welcome. (to a female)	**Bienvenida.**
	(b'yen-beh-NEE-thah)
Welcome. (to an all-male or mixed group)	**Bienvenidos.**
	(b'yen-beh-NEE-thohs)
Welcome. (to an all-female group)	**Bienvenidas.**
	(b'yen-beh-NEE-thahs)

Pleasantries

Just as "Hi, how are you?" is usually the first thing we say when we greet each other in English, its equivalent in Spanish is the most usual greeting.

How are you?	**¿Cómo está?**
	(KOHM-weh-STAH)

To say the same thing to more than one person, just add **n** to **está**, resulting in **están**:

How are you (all)?	**¿Cómo están?**
	(KOHM-weh-STAHN)

Here are some stock answers:

Fine, thank you.	**Bien, gracias.**
	(B'YEN GRAH-s'yahs)
So-so.	**Regular.**
	(reh-goo-LAHR)
	Más o menos. (lit.: more or less)
	(MAHS oh MEH-nos)
Not well.	**Mal.**
	(MAHL)

Family and Friends

"Family first" is an important concept in Hispanic culture, and asking about the health of family members is one way to show that you understand and appreciate this.

Use the following formula to ask about one person:

How is your <u>mother</u>?	**¿Cómo está su <u>mamá</u>?**
	(KOHM-weh-STAH soo mah-MAH)

Just substitute any of the following words to ask about others:

father	**papá**
	(pah-PAH)
husband	**esposo**
	(eh-SPOH-soh)

wife	**esposa**
	(eh-SPOH-sah)
sister	**hermana**
	(ehr-MAH-nah)
brother	**hermano**
	(ehr-MAH-noh)
son	**hijo**
	(EE-hoh)
daughter	**hija**
	(EE-hah)

To inquire about more than one person at a time, just add **s** to **su**, another **s** to make the word plural, and add **n** to **está**:

How are your <u>parents</u>?	**¿Cómo están sus papás?**
	(KOHM-weh-STAHN soos pah-PAHS)
children	**hijos**
	(EE-hohs)
daughters	**hijas**
	(EE-hahs)
sisters and brothers	**hermanos**
	(ehr-MAH-nohs)
sisters	**hermanas**
	(ehr-MAH-nahs)

While we're on the subject of people important to us, let's include a few more whom we can't do without:

friend (male)	**amigo**
	(ah-MEE-goh)

friend (female)	**amiga**
	(ah-MEE-gah)
coworker	**colega**
	(koh-LEH-gah)
(male)	**compañero**
	(kohm-pahn-YEH-roh)
(female)	**compañera**
	(kohm-pahn-YEH-rah)
boyfriend	**novio**
	(NOH-b'yoh)
girlfriend	**novia**
	(NOH-b'yah)
boss (male)	**patrón / jefe**
	(pah-TROHN) / (HEH-feh)
boss (female)	**patrona / jefa**
	(pah-TROH-nah) / (HEH-fah)
neighbor (male)	**vecino**
	(beh-SEE-noh)
neighbor (female)	**vecina**
	(beh-SEE-nah)

These words can also be made plural by adding **s** (or **es** in the case of **patrón**).

The "Magic" Words

These are the essential words for showing courtesy and respect. Memorize these right away.

Please.	**Por favor.**
	(por fah-BOR)
Thank you.	**Gracias.**
	(GRAH-s'yahs)
You're welcome.	**De nada.**
	(deh NAH-thah)
Excuse me.	**Disculpe.**
	(dee-SKOOL-peh)
I'm sorry.	**Lo siento.**
	(loh S'YEN-toh)

Telling Present Time and Using Numbers 1–12

In the following section, you will find phrases for asking and telling time. The numbers from 1 to 12, which you will need for other purposes as well, are introduced here.

What time is it?	**¿Qué hora es?**
	(KEH OR-ah ess)

This question is answered for *one o'clock* by the phrase:

It's one o'clock.	**Es la una.**
	(ess lah OO-nah)

For all other hours, use the following phrase, inserting a number between two and twelve:

It's <u>two</u> o'clock.	**Son las <u>dos</u>.**
	(sohn lahs DOHS)

Spanish Basics

three	**tres**
	(TRESS)
four	**cuatro**
	(K'WAH-troh)
five	**cinco**
	(SEENG-koh)
six	**seis**
	(SACE) (rhymes with *face*)
seven	**siete**
	(S'YEH-teh)
eight	**ocho**
	(OH-choh)
nine	**nueve**
	(N'WEH-beh)
ten	**diez**
	(D'YESS)
eleven	**once**
	(OHN-seh)
twelve	**doce**
	(DOH-seh)

For times in between the hours, use the following expressions:

It's one-fifteen.	**Es la una y cuarto.**
	(ess lah OO-nah ee K'WAHR-toh)
It's two-thirty.	**Son las dos y media.**
	(sohn lahs DOHS ee MEH-th'yah)
It's three-forty-five.	**Son las tres y cuarenta y cinco.**
	(sohn lahs TRESS ee kwah-REN-tah ee SEENG-koh)

You can express *noon* and *midnight* as follows:

It's twelve o'clock noon.	**Es mediodía.**
	(ess meh-th'yoh-DEE-ah)
It's midnight.	**Es medianoche.**
	(ess meh-th'yah-NOH-cheh)

To indicate *morning*, add **de la mañana** to any hour:

It's ten A.M.	**Son las diez de la mañana.**
	(sohn lahs D'YESS deh lah mahn-YAH-nah)

For *afternoon* or *evening*, add **de la tarde**:

It's four P.M.	**Son las cuatro de la tarde.**
	(sohn lahs K'WAH-troh deh lah TAHR-deh)

For *night*, add **de la noche**:

It's nine P.M.	**Son las nueve de la noche.**
	(sohn lahs N'WEH-beh deh lah NOH-cheh)

Talking to More than One Person at a Time

To give instructions to a group of people, just add **n** to the main word:

Come. (to one person)	**Venga.**
	(BENG-gah)
Come. (to two or more people)	**Vengan.**
	(BENG-gahn)
Be here. (to one person)	**Esté aquí.**
	(eh-STEH ah-KEE)
Be here. (to two or more people)	**Estén aquí.**
	(eh-STEN ah-KEE)

Days of the Week

If you look at a Spanish calendar, you will see that the extreme left-hand column is for Monday, rather than Sunday, as in North American calendars. Sunday is put in the extreme right-hand column, putting the weekend days together. Most workers expect one free day a week, and not necessarily on a weekend. This day is often referred to by workers as **mi día** (*my day*).

What day is today?	**¿Qué día es hoy?**
	(KEH DEE-ah ess OY)
Today is <u>Monday</u>.	**Hoy es <u>lunes</u>.**
	(OY ess LOO-ness)
Tomorrow is <u>Tuesday</u>.	**Mañana es <u>martes</u>.**
	(mahn-YAH-nah ess MAHR-tess)
Wednesday	**miércoles**
	(M'YEHR-koh-less)
Thursday	**jueves**
	(H'WEH-bess)
Friday	**viernes**
	(B'YER-ness)

Saturday	**sábado**
	(SAH-bah-thoh)
Sunday	**domingo**
	(doh-MEENG-goh)

To indicate a day in the future, add **el** before the name of the day:

Be here on Monday.	**Esté aquí el lunes.**
	(eh-STEH ah-KEE el LOO-ness)

To indicate *always on that day* add **los** before the name of the day:

Come on Mondays.	**Venga los lunes.**
	(BENG-gah lohs LOO-ness)
Come every day.	**Venga todos los días.**
	(BENG-gah TOH-thohs lohs DEE-ahs)
Don't come on Sundays.	**No venga los domingos.**
	(NOH BENG-gah lohs doh-MEENG-gohs)

Months of the Year and Using Numbers 1–31

Did you notice that the days of the week are not capitalized in Spanish? Neither are the months. Also, when giving the date in abbreviated form in Spanish, it is exactly the opposite from English. Thus, 3/9/07 in English would be March 9, 2007. In Spanish, it would be September 3, 2007. Let's look at how these dates are written and said.

Spanish Basics

What's the date?	**¿Cuál es la fecha?**
	(KWAHL ess lah FEH-cha)
It's the <u>first</u> of <u>January</u>.	**Es el <u>primero</u> de <u>enero</u>.**
	(ess el pree-MEH-roh deh eh-NEH-roh)

After "the first" day, the dates are given in cardinal numbers, as in "the 'two' of January," "the 'three' of January," and so forth. The following examples use all of the months and numbers up to thirty-one.

It's <u>the second</u> of <u>January</u>.	**Es el <u>dos</u> de <u>enero</u>.**
	(ess el DOHS deh eh-NEH-roh)
the third of February	**el tres de febrero**
	(el TRESS deh feh-BREH-roh)
the fourth of March	**el cuatro de marzo**
	(el K'WAH-troh deh MAHR-soh)
the fifth of April	**el cinco de abril**
	(el SEENG-koh deh ah-BREEL)
the sixth of May	**el seis de mayo**
	(el SACE de MAH-yoh)
the seventh of June	**el siete de junio**
	(el S'YEH-teh deh HOON-yoh)
the eighth of July	**el ocho de julio**
	(el OH-choh de HOOL-yoh)
the ninth of August	**el nueve de agosto**
	(el N'WEH-beh deh ah-GOH-stoh)
the tenth of September	**el diez de septiembre**
	(el D'YESS deh sep-T'YEM-breh)

the eleventh of October — **el once de octubre**
(el OHN-seh deh ohk-
    TOO-breh)

the twelfth of November — **el doce de noviembre**
(el DOH-seh deh noh-
    B'YEM-breh)

the thirteenth of December — **el trece de diciembre**
(el TREH-seh deh dee-
    S'YEM-breh)

the fourteenth — **el catorce**
(el kah-TOR-seh)

the fifteenth — **el quince**
(el KEEN-seh)

the sixteenth — **el dieciséis**
(el d'yes-ee-SACE)

the seventeenth — **el diecisiete**
(el d'yes-ee S'YEH-teh)

the eighteenth — **el dieciocho**
(el d'yes-YOH-choh)

the nineteenth — **el diecinueve**
(el d'yes-ee-N'WEH-beh)

the twentieth — **el veinte**
(el BAYN-teh)

the twenty-first — **el veintiuno**
(el bayn-T'YOO-noh)

the twenty-second — **el veintidós**
(el bayn-tee-DOHS)

the twenty-third — **el veintitrés**
(el bayn-tee-TRESS)

the twenty-fourth	**el veinticuatro** (el bayn-tee-K'WAH-troh)
the twenty-fifth	**el veinticinco** (el bayn-tee-SEENG-koh)
the twenty-sixth	**el veintiséis** (el bayn-tee-SACE)
the twenty-seventh	**el veintisiete** (el bayn-tee-S'YEH-teh)
the twenty-eighth	**el veintiocho** (el bayn-T'YOH-choh)
the twenty-ninth	**el veintinueve** (el bayn-tee-N'WEH-beh)
the thirtieth	**el treinta** (el TRAIN-tah)
the thirty-first	**el treinta y uno** (el train-tie-OO-noh)

Talking About the Weather

Sometimes talking about the weather is more than just a pleasantry—the weather can affect the work planned for day. Here are some common weather expressions.

How's the weather?	**¿Qué tiempo hace?** (KEH T'YEM-poh AH-seh)
It's fine.	**Hace buen tiempo.** (AH-seh B'WEHN T'YEM-poh)
It's hot.	**Hace calor.** (AH-seh kah-LOR)

It's cold.	**Hace frío.**
	(AH-seh FREE-oh)
It's raining.	**Está lloviendo.**
	(eh-STAH yoh-B'YEN-doh)
It's snowing.	**Está nevando.**
	(eh-STAH neh-BAHN-doh)
It's windy.	**Hace viento.**
	(AH-seh B'YEN-toh)
It's sunny.	**Hace sol.**
	(AH-seh SOHL)
It's cloudy.	**Está nublado.**
	(eh-STAH noo-BLAH-thoh)
There's a storm.	**Hay una tormenta.**
	(EYE OO-nah tor-MEN-tah)

Interviewing an Employee

The following phrases will help you learn the most basic information about your prospective employees.

What's your name?	**¿Cuál es su nombre?**
	(K'WAHL ess soo NOHM-breh)
Where are you from?	**¿De dónde es?**
	(deh THOHN-deh ess?)
Where do you live?	**¿Dónde vive?**
	(DOHN-deh BEE-beh)
How long have you lived here?	**¿Hace cuánto que vive aquí?**
	(AH-seh K'WAHN-toh keh BEE-beh
	ah-KEE)

Where did you work before?	**¿Dónde trabajó antes?**
	(DOHN-deh trah-bah-HOH AHN-tess)
What kind of work did you do?	**¿Qué tipo de trabajo hizo?**
	(KEH TEE-poh deh trah-BAH-hoh EE-soh)
Do you have any experience in <u>construction</u>?	**¿Tiene experiencia en construcción?**
	(T'YEH-neh ex-pehr-YEN-s'yah en kohn- strook-S'YOHN)
Have you worked as a <u>plumber</u> before?	**¿Ha trabajado como <u>plomero</u> alguna vez?**
	(ah trah-bah-HAH-thoh koh-moh ploh-MEH-roh ahl-goo-nah BESS)

Asking for References

Notice that the question about contacting "her" is exactly the same as the one about contacting "you" when you are speaking to a female. Likewise, the question about "him" is the same as the one about "you" when you are speaking to a male.

Can you give me a reference?	**¿Me puede dar una referencia?**
	(meh PWEH-theh dahr oo-nah reh-feh-REN-s'yah)
How can I contact her / you?	**¿Cómo la puedo contactar?**
	(KOH-moh lah PWEH-thoh kohn-tahk-TAHR)
How can I contact him / you?	**¿Cómo lo puedo contactar?**
	(KOH-moh loh PWEH-thoh kohn-tahk-TAHR)

Hiring an Employee

The following basic phrases will help you establish a relationship with a new employee.

You're hired. (to a female)	**Usted está contratada.**
	(oo-STED eh-STAH kohn-trah-TAH-thah)
You're hired. (to a male)	**Usted está contratado.**
	(oo-STED eh-STAH kohn-trah-TAH-thoh)
You're hired. (to a group)	**Ustedes están contratados.**
	(oo-STEH-thes eh-STAHN kohn-trah-TAH-thohs)

Scheduling

Here are some phrases that will help you establish days and hours of work. To substitute different days and times, find the suitable words on the preceding pages.

Can you come . . .	**¿Puede venir...**
	(PWEH-theh beh-NEER)
every day?	**todos los días?**
	(TOH-thohs lohs DEE-ahs)
every week?	**cada semana?**
	(KAH-thah seh-MAH-nah)
from Monday through Friday?	**de lunes a viernes?**
	(de LOO-ness ah B'YEHR-ness)

once a week?	**una vez a la semana?**
	(oo-nah BESS ah lah seh-MAH-nah)
on <u>Mondays</u>?	**los <u>lunes</u>?**
	(lohs LOO-ness)
twice a week?	**dos veces a la semana?**
	(DOHS BEH-sess ah lah seh-MAH-nah)
once a month?	**una vez al mes?**
	(oo-nah BESS ahl MESS)
twice a month?	**dos veces al mes?**
	(DOHS BEH-sess ahl MESS)
<u>four</u> hours a day?	**<u>cuatro</u> horas al día?**
	(K'WAH-troh OR-ahs ahl DEE-ah)
<u>thirty</u> hours a week?	**<u>treinta</u> horas a la semana?**
	(TRAIN-tah OR-ahs ah lah seh-MAH-nah)
when I need extra help?	**cuando necesite ayuda extra?**
	(kwan-doh neh-seh-SEE-teh ah-YOO-thah EX-trah)

Discussing Salary and Using Numbers 40+

It's important to establish how you will pay your employees right at the beginning. Review the numbers between 1 and 31 on page 157. Higher numbers are introduced on the pages that follow.

Perfect Phrases in Spanish for Construction

Your wages will be . . .	**Su sueldo será...**
	(soo SWELL-doh seh-RAH)
<u>ten</u> dollars an hour	**diez dólares por hora**
	(D'YESS DOH-lah-ress por
	OR-ah)
<u>forty</u> dollars for four hours	**cuarenta dólares por cuatro horas**
	(k'wah-REN-tah DOH-lah-ress
	por K'WAH-troh OR-ahs)
forty-five	**cuarenta y cinco**
	(k'wah-REN-tie SEENG-koh)
fifty	**cincuenta**
	(seeng-KWEN-tah)
sixty	**sesenta**
	(seh-SEN-tah)
seventy	**setenta**
	(seh-TEN-tah)
eighty	**ochenta**
	(oh-CHEN-tah)
ninety	**noventa**
	(noh-BEN-tah)
one hundred	**cien**
	(S'YEN)
one hundred and fifty	**ciento cincuenta**
	(S'YEN-toh seeng-K'WEN-tah)
two hundred	**doscientos**
	(dohs-S'YEN-tohs)
three hundred	**trescientos**
	(tress-S'YEN-tohs)

four hundred	**cuatrocientos**
	(k'wah-troh S'YEN-tohs)
five hundred	**quinientos**
	(keen-YEN-tohs)
six hundred	**seiscientos**
	(sace-S'YEN-tohs)
seven hundred	**setecientos**
	(seh-teh S'YEN-tohs)
eight hundred	**ochocientos**
	(oh-choh S'YEN-tohs)
nine hundred	**novecientos**
	(noh-beh S'YEN-tohs)
one thousand	**mil**
	(MEEL)
two thousand	**dos mil**
	(DOHS MEEL)

You may have noticed that the numbers sixteen to nineteen are each written as one word (**dieciséis**, **diecisiete**, etc.) even though their literal meaning is "ten and six," "ten and seven," and so on. The same is true for the numbers twenty-one to twenty-nine: **veintiuno** (twenty and one), **veintidós** (twenty and two), and so on. Beginning with the thirties, and up to ninety-nine, similar combinations are written as three words:

thirty-one	**treinta y uno**
	(train-tie OO-noh)
forty-two	**cuarenta y dos**
	(k'wah-REN-tie DOHS)

fifty-three	**cincuenta y tres**
	(seeng-KWEN-tie TRESS)
sixty-four	**sesenta y cuatro**
	(seh-SEN-tie K'WAH-troh)
seventy-five	**setenta y cinco**
	(seh-TEN-tie SEENG-koh)
eighty-six	**ochenta y seis**
	(oh-CHEN-tie SACE)
ninety-seven	**noventa y siete**
	(noh-BEN-tie S'YEH-teh)

The **y** (*and*) is important in these combinations. In contrast, while we often use *and* with hundreds in English, **y** is never used with hundreds in Spanish:

a hundred (and) ten	**ciento diez**
	(S'YEN-toh D'YESS)
four hundred (and) sixty	**cuatrocientos sesenta**
	(KWAH-troh S'YEN-tohs seh-SEN-tah)
five hundred and seventy-five	**quinientos setenta y cinco**
	(keen-YEN-tohs seh-TEN-tie
	SEENG-koh)

Rates of Payment

The following phrases tell how to express "per" a period of time.

per hour	**por hora**
	(por OR-ah)
per day	**por día**
	(por DEE-ah)

per week	**por semana**
	(por seh-MAH-nah)
per month	**por mes**
	(por MESS)
for the completed job	**por el trabajo completado**
	(por el trah-BAH-hoh kohm- pleh-TAH-thoh)

Discussing Pay Periods

Making the following clear to an employee at the beginning will help avoid misunderstandings.

I'll pay you . . .	**Le pagaré...**
	(leh pah-gah-REH)
at the end of each day.	**al fin de cada día.**
	(ahl FEEN deh KAH-thah DEE-ah)
at the end of the week.	**al fin de la semana.**
	(ahl FEEN deh lah seh- MAH-nah)
when you finish the job.	**cuando termine el trabajo.**
	(k'wan-doh tehr-MEE-neh el trah-BAH-hoh)
by check.	**con cheque.**
	(kohn CHEH-keh)
in cash.	**en efectivo.**
	(en eh-fek-TEE-boh)
I cannot pay you . . .	**No le puedo pagar...**
	(NOH leh P'WEH-thoh pah-GAHR)

in advance.	**por adelantado.**
	(por ah-theh-lahn-TAH-thoh)
before the job is finished.	**antes que se termine el**
	trabajo.
	(AHN-tess keh seh tehr-MEE-nehl tra-BAH-hoh)

Discussing Taxes

The phrases in this section will help you make it clear whether you wish to pay your employee's taxes or expect him to pay his own.

I will pay your Social Security taxes.	**Yo pagaré sus impuestos de**
	Seguridad Social.
	(YOH pah-gah-REH soos eem-PWEH-stohs deh seh-goo-ree-THAD soh-S'YAHL)
You must pay your own Social Security taxes.	**Usted debe pagar sus propios**
	impuestos de Seguridad Social.
	(oo-STED deh-beh pah-GAHR soos PROH-p'yohs eem-PWEH-stohs deh seh-goo-ree-THAD soh-S'YAHL)
You must pay your own income taxes.	**Usted debe pagar los impuestos**
	por sus ingresos.
	(oo-STED deh-beh pah-GAHR lohs eem-PWEH-stohs por soos een-GREH-sohs)
I will help you with the documents.	**Yo lo ayudaré con los documentos.**
	(YOH loh ah-yoo-thah-REH kohn lohs doh-koo-MEN-tohs)

I cannot help you with the documents.	**No puedo ayudarlo con los documentos.**
	(NOH PWEH-thoh ah-yoo-THAHR-loh kohn lohs doh-koo-MEN-tohs)

Showing Appreciation for Good Work

The following are phrases everyone likes to hear.

You did a good job.	**Ha hecho buen trabajo.**
	(ah EH-choh B'WEN trah-BAH-hoh)
You did a great job.	**Hizo el trabajo muy bien.**
	(EE-soh el trah-BAH-hoh M'WEE B'YEN)
You are punctual.	**Usted es muy puntual.**
	(oo-STED ess m'wee poon-TWAHL)
I'm happy with your work.	**Me gusta su trabajo.**
	(meh GOO-stah soo trah-BAH-hoh)
I'm raising your salary.	**Voy a aumentar su sueldo.**
	(boy ah ah'oo-men-TAHR soo SWELL-doh)
I am paying you extra today.	**Hoy le doy algo extra.**
	(OY leh doy ahl-goh EX-trah)

Clearing Up Confusion

Be sure to tell your employees what to do if they have a problem or an emergency situation.

Call me if you cannot come.	**Llámeme si no puede venir.**
	(YAH-meh-meh see noh PWEH-theh beh-NEER)
In an emergency, call me.	**Si hay una emergencia, llámeme.**
	(see eye oo-nah eh-mehr-HEN-s'yah YAH-meh-meh)
My telephone number is: 202-769-5416.	**Mi teléfono es dos cero dos, siete seis nueve, cinco cuatro uno seis.**
	(mee teh-LEH-foh-noh ess DOHS SEH-roh DOHS S'YEH-teh SACE N'WEH-beh SEENG-koh K'WAH-troh OO-noh SACE)
Tell me if you have a problem.	**Dígame si tiene algún problema.**
	(DEE-gah-meh see T'YEH-neh ahl-GOON proh-BLEH-mah)
Tell me if you do not understand.	**Dígame si no entiende.**
	(DEE-gah-meh see NOH en-T'YEN-deh)

Terminating an Employee

The following are phrases nobody wants to hear, but sometimes they are necessary.

I no longer need you. (to a male)	**Ya no lo necesito.**
	(YAH noh loh neh-seh-SEE-toh)
I no longer need you. (to a female)	**Ya no la necesito.**
	(YAH noh lah neh-seh-SEE-toh)

Spanish Basics

You are fired. (to a male)	**Usted está despedido.**
	(oo-STED eh-STAH dess-peh-THEE-thoh)
You are fired. (to a female)	**Usted está despedida.**
	(oo-STED eh-STAH dess-peh-THEE-thah)
Because . . .	**Porque...**
	(POR-keh)
you didn't do the job well.	**no hizo bien el trabajo.**
	(NOH EE-soh B'YEN el trah-BAH-hoh)
you didn't come when I expected you.	**no vino cuando yo la (lo) esperaba.**
	(NOH BEE-noh kwan-doh yoh lah [loh] eh-speh-RAH-bah)
you never came on time.	**nunca llegó a tiempo.**
	(NOONG-kah yeh-GOH ah T'YEM-poh)
you work too slowly.	**trabaja muy lento.**
	(trah-BAH-hah m'wee LEN-toh)
you don't have the necessary skills.	**no tiene las habilidades necesarias.**
	(NOH T'YEH-neh lahs ah-beel-ee-THAH-thess neh-seh-SAHR-yahs)
you didn't follow instructions.	**no siguió las instrucciones.**
	(NOH see-G'YOH lahs een-strook-S'YOH-ness)

you broke a lot of things.	**rompió muchas cosas.**
	(rohm-P'YOH MOO-chahs KOH-sahs)
you don't get along with the other workers.	**no se lleva bien con los otros trabajadores.**
	(NOH seh YEH-bah B'YEN kohn lohs oh-trohs trah-bah-hah-THOR ess)
the supervisor.	**el supervisor.**
	(el soo-pehr-bee-SOR)
you have a bad attitude.	**tiene mala actitud.**
	(T'YEH-neh MAH-lah ahk-tee-TOOD)
you smoked on the job.	**fumó mientras trabajaba.**
	(foo-MOH m'yen-trahs trah-bah-HAH-bah)
you came to work drunk.	**vino borracho al trabajo.**
	(BEE-noh bor-RAH-choh ahl trah-BAH-hoh)
you drank alcohol on the job.	**tomó alcohol mientras trabajaba.**
	(toh-MOH ahl-KOHL M'YEN-trahs trah-bah-HAH-bah)
I no longer need you.	**ya no lo necesito.**
	(YAH NOH loh neh-seh-SEE-toh)

Basic Questions and Answers

In this section you will learn how to form *yes-or-no* questions as well as those that begin with question words like *who*, *where*, *when*, and so on. Typical answers are also provided.

Yes-or-No *Questions*

A *yes-or-no* (**sí o no**) question in Spanish is made by pronouncing a statement as a question. For example:

End a statement on the same tone you began on.

You have the money.	**Tiene el dinero.**
	(T'YEH-neh el dee-NEH-roh)

End a question on a tone higher than the one you began on.

Do you have the money?	**¿Tiene el dinero?**
	(t'yeh-neh el dee-NEH-roh)

It would be especially polite to include the person's name in answering this type of question:

Yes, Carlos.	**Sí, Carlos.**
	(SEE KAHR-lohs)
No, Juan.	**No, Juan.**
	(NOH H'WAHN)
Maybe.	**Quizás.**
	(kee-SAHS)
It depends.	**Depende.**
	(de-PEN-deh)

God willing!

¡Ojalá!

(oh-ha-LAH)

Information Questions

The following general questions and possible answers are included to help you request or provide information.

Who . . . ?	**¿Quién?**
	(K'YEN)
I	**yo**
	(YOH)
you	**usted**
	(oo-STED)
he	**él**
	(el)
she	**ella**
	(EH-yah)
we (in a mixed or all-male combination)	**nosotros** (noh-SOH-trohs)
we (when both or all are female)	**nosotras** (noh-SOH-trahs)
you all	**ustedes** (oo-STEH-thes)
they (when mixed or all male)	**ellos** (EH-yohs)
they (when all are female)	**ellas** (EH-yahs)
Who with?	**¿Con quién?** (kohn K'YEN)

with me	**conmigo**
	(kohn MEE-goh)
with you	**con usted**
	(kohn oo-STED)
with him	**con él**
	(kohn el)
with her	**con ella**
	(kohn EH-yah)
with them	con **ellos/ellas**
	(kohn EH-yohs/EH-yahs)
Whose is it?	**¿De quién es?**
	(deh K'YEN ess)
It's mine.	**Es mío.**
	(ess MEE-oh)
It's yours/ his/ hers/ theirs.	**Es suyo.**
	(ess SOO-yoh)
What is it?	**¿Qué es?**
	(KEH ess)
It's <u>this</u>.	**Es <u>esto</u>.**
	(ess EH-stoh)
that	**eso**
	(EH-soh)
Where is it?	**¿Dónde está?**
	(DOHN-deh eh-STAH)
It's <u>here</u>.	**Está <u>aquí</u>.**
	(eh-STAH ah-KEE)
there	**ahí**
	(ah-EE)
over there	**allí**
	(ah-YEE)

Where are you going?	**¿Adónde va?**
	(ah-THOHN-deh bah)
I'm going <u>home</u>.	**Voy a casa.**
	(BOY ah KAH-sah)
to the supermarket.	**al supermercado.**
	(al soo-pehr-mehr-KAH-thoh)
When?	**¿Cuándo?**
	(KWAHN-doh)
now	**ahora**
	(ah-OR-ah)
later	**más tarde**
	(MAHS TAHR-deh)
soon	**pronto**
	(PROHN-toh)
always	**siempre**
	(S'YEM-preh)
never	**nunca**
	(NOONG-kah)
Until when?	**¿Hasta cuándo?**
	(AH-stah KWAHN-doh)
Until <u>Monday</u>.	**Hasta el <u>lunes</u>.**
	(AH-stah el LOO-ness)
Until <u>three</u> o'clock.	**Hasta las <u>tres</u>.**
	(AH-stah lahs TRESS)
How?	**¿Cómo?**
	(KOH-moh)
Like this / Like that.	**Así.**
	(ah-SEE)
For how long?	**¿Por cuánto tiempo?**
	(por KWAHN-toh T'YEM-poh)

Spanish Basics

For two hours.

Por dos horas.

(por dohs OR-ahs)

A few minutes.

Unos pocos minutos.

(oo-nohs poh-kohs mee-
NOO-tohs)

How many are there?

¿Cuántos hay?

(K'WAHN-tohs EYE)

There is one.

Hay uno.

(eye OO-noh)

There are two.

Hay dos.

(eye DOHS)

There are a lot.

Hay muchos.

(eye MOO-chohs)

a few

unos pocos

(oo-nohs POH-kohs)

How much is it?

¿Cuánto es?

(KWAHN-toh ess)

It's twenty dollars.

Son veinte dólares.

(sohn BAYN-teh DOH-lah-ress)

It's a lot.

Es mucho.

(ess MOO-choh)

only a little

muy poco

(m'wee POH-koh)

Chapter 2

Establishing Basic Policies

Selecting Workers

The following phrases will help you select the kind of workers you need.

I need <u>laborers</u>.	**Necesito <u>obreros</u>.**
	(neh-seh-SEE-toh oh-BREH-rohs)
skilled workers	**trabajadores hábiles**
	(trah-bah-hah-THOR-ess
	AH-bee-less)
carpenters	**carpinteros**
	(kar-peen-TEH-rohs)
roofers	**constructores de techos**
	(kohn-strook-TOR-ess deh
	TEH-chohs)
electricians	**electricistas**
	(eh-lek-tree-SEE-stahs)
plumbers	**plomeros**
	(ploh-MEH-rohs)

HVAC technicians	**técnicos de calefacción y aire acondicionado** (TEK-nee-kohs deh kah-leh-fak-S'YOHN ee eye-reh ah-kon dee-s'yoh-NAH-thoh)
painters	**pintores** (peen-TOR-ess)
window installers	**instaladores de ventanas** (een-stah-lah-THOR-ess deh ben-TAH-nahs)
appliance installers	**instaladores de electrodomésticos** (een-stah-lah-THOR-ess deh eh-lek-troh-doh-MESS-tee-kohs)
tile setters	**expertos en azulejos y losas** (eks-PEHR-tohs en ah-soo-LEH-hohs ee LOH-sahs)
carpet and vinyl flooring installers	**instaladores de alfombras y pisos de vinil** (een-stah-lah-THOR-ess deh ahl-FOHM-brahs ee PEE-sohs deh bee-NEEL)
hardwood flooring installers	**instaladores de pisos de madera** (een-stah-lah-THOR-ess deh PEE-sohs deh mah-THEH-rah)
refinishers	**renovadores** (reh-noh-bah-THOR-ess)

truck drivers	**conductores de camión**
	(kohn-dook-TOR-ess deh kahm-YOHN)
heavy equipment operators	**operadores de equipo pesado**
	(oh-peh-rah-THOR-ess deh eh-KEE-poh peh-SAH-thoh)
mechanics	**mecánicos**
	(meh-KAH-nee-kohs)
landscapers	**jardineros**
	(har-dee-NEH-rohs)
bricklayers	**albañiles**
	(ahl-bahn-YEE-less)
ditchdiggers	**excavadores**
	(ek-skah-bah-THOR-ess)
unskilled laborers	**obreros sin especializaciones**
	(oh-BREH-rohs seen eh-speh-s'yah-lee-sah-S'YOH-ness)
I have work for unskilled laborers for . . .	**Tengo trabajo para obreros sin especializaciones para...**
	(teng-goh trah-BAH-hoh pah-rah oh-BREH-rohs seen eh-speh-s'yah-lee-sah-S'YOH-ness pah-rah)
heavy lifting.	**levantar objetos pesados.**
	(leh-bahn-TAHR ohb-HEH-tohs peh-SAH-thohs)
digging.	**excavar.**
	(eks-kah-BAHR)
clearing brush.	**sacar la hierba mala.**
	(sah-KAHR lah YEHR-bah MAH-lah)

roadwork.	**trabajar en las carreteras.** (trah-bah-HAHR en las kahr-reh-TEH-rahs)
cleaning up.	**limpiar.** (leemp-YAHR)
various jobs.	**hacer varios trabajos.** (ah-SEHR BAHR-yohs trah- BAH-hohs)

Certification and Training

The following phrases will help you make sure your prospective employees have the proper certification and training for certain jobs.

To do this job, you need . . .	**Para hacer este trabajo, usted** **necesita...** (pah-rah ah-SER eh-steh trah-BAH- hoh oo-STED neh-seh-SEE-tah)
a driver's license. (commercial)	**un permiso de manejar.** **(comercial)** (oon pehr-MEE-soh deh mah-neh-HAR [koh- mehr-S'YAHL])
certification to use <u>certain</u> <u>equipment</u>.	**certificación para usar** **ciertos aparatos.** (ser-tee-fee-kah-S'YOHN pah-rah oo-SAHR S'YEHR- tohs ah-pah-RAH-tohs)
motorized equipment	**maquinaria motorizada** (mah-kee-NAHR-yah moh-tor-ee-SAH-thah)

Do you have certification?	**¿Tiene certificación?**
	(T'YEH-neh ser-tee-fee-kah-S'YOHN)
a license	**una licencia**
	(oo-nah lee-SENSE-yah)
To get certification . . .	**Para obtener la certificación...**
	(pah-rah ohb-teh-NEHR lah
	ser-tee-fee-kah-S'YOHN)
you need to take a training course.	**usted necesita hacer un curso de entrenamiento.**
	(oo-STED neh-seh-SEE-tah
	ah-SEHR oon KOOR-soh deh
	en-treh-nah-M'YEN-toh)
go to this address	**ir a esta dirección**
	(EER ah EH-stah dee-rek-S'YOHN)
call this number	**llamar a este número**
	(yah-MAHR ah EH-steh NOO-meh-roh)
come here tomorrow	**venir acá mañana**
	(beh-NEER ah-KAH mahn-YAH-nah)
I'll take you.	**Yo lo llevo.**
	(YOH loh YEH-boh)

Establishing a Work Schedule

How long should a job, task, or project last? How long do you want someone to wait before doing something else? Use the following expressions to explain what you want. You can consult a complete overview of numbers in Spanish on page 157–159 to help specify a particular time period.

This job . . .	**Este trabajo...**
	(EH-steh trah-BAH-hoh)
project	**proyecto**
	(proh-YEK-toh)
task / chore	**tarea**
	(tah-REH-ah)
will last all day.	**durará todo el día.**
	(doo-rah-RAH toh-thoh el DEE-ah)
for a short time	**un tiempo corto**
	(oon T'YEM-poh KOR-toh)
a long time	**un tiempo largo**
	(oon T'YEM-poh LAHR-goh)
five minutes	**cinco minutos**
	(SEENG-koh mee-NOO-tohs)
an hour	**una hora**
	(OO-nah OH-rah)
two hours	**dos horas**
	(DOHS OR-ahs)
a week	**una semana**
	(OO-nah seh-MAH-nah)
a month	**un mes**
	(OON MESS)
a year	**un año**
	(OON AHN-yoh)

Planning the Day

The following phrases will help you tell your employees where to be, and at what time. They will also help you tell them what to do about meals and breaks during the day.

I will meet you <u>here</u>.	**Nos veremos aquí.**
	(nohs beh-REH-mohs ah-KEE)
I will pick you up <u>here</u>.	**Lo recojo aquí.**
	(loh reh-KOH-hoh ah-KEE)
at the bus stop	**en la parada de autobuses**
	(en lah pah-RAH-thah deh ah'oo-toh-BOO-sess)
at the train station	**en la estación de trenes**
	(en lah eh-stahs-YOHN deh TREH-ness)
at the metro station	**en la estación del metro**
	(en lah eh-stahs-YOHN del MEH-troh)
on the corner	**en la esquina**
	(en lah eh-SKEE-nah)
in the parking lot	**en el parqueo**
	(en el pahr-KEH-oh)
Be here at six A.M. tomorrow.	**Esté aquí mañana a las seis de la mañana.**
	(eh-STEH ah-KEE mahn-YAH-nah ah lahs SACE deh lah mahn-YAH-nah)

You will have a twenty-minute break at 9:30.	**Tiene un descanso de veinte minutos a las nueve y media.**
	(T'YEH-neh oon dess-KAHN-soh deh BAYN-teh mee-NOO-tohs ah las N'WEH-beh ee MEH-th'yah)
You have a <u>one-hour</u> break for lunch.	**Tiene <u>una hora</u> para almorzar.**
	(T'YEH-neh OO-nah OR-ah pah-rah ahl-mor-SAHR)
half-hour	**media hora**
	(MEH-th'yah OR-ah)
You can buy <u>your lunch</u> nearby.	**Puede comprar <u>su almuerzo</u> cerca del sitio de trabajo.**
	(PWEH-theh kohm-prahr soo ahl-M'WEHR-soh SEHR-kah del SEET-yoh deh trah-BAH-hoh)
soft drinks	**refrescos**
	(reh-FRESS-kohs)
coffee	**café**
	(kah-FEH)
Bring your own lunch.	**Traiga su propio almuerzo.**
	(TRY-gah soo PROH-p'yoh ahl-M'WEHR-soh)
The restrooms are <u>here</u>.	**Los baños están <u>aquí</u>.**
	(lohs BAHN-yohs eh-stahn ah-KEE)
over there	**allí**
	(ah-YEE)
inside	**adentro**
	(ah-THEN-troh)

We will come back here at 4:30.	**Regresaremos aquí a las cuatro y media.**
	(reh-greh-sah-REH-mohs ah-KEE ah lahs KWAH-troh ee MEH-th'yah)
You may leave at 5:00.	**Usted puede irse a las cinco.**
	(oo-STED pweh-theh EER-seh ah lahs SEENG-koh)
I'll see you tomorrow.	**Hasta mañana.**
	(AH-stah mahn-YAH-nah)
Same time, same place.	**A la misma hora, en el mismo lugar.**
	(ah lah MEEZ-mah OR-ah en el MEEZ-moh loo-GAHR)
Smoking is prohibited here.	**Se prohíbe fumar aquí.**
	(seh proh-EE-beh foo-MAHR ah-KEE)
You may smoke in this area.	**Se puede fumar en esta área.**
	(seh PWEH-theh foo-MAHR en EH-steh AH-reh-ah)

Job Locations

The following expressions will help you indicate exactly where the project will take place.

The construction site is in the city.	**El sitio de construcción está en la ciudad.**
	(el SEE-t'yoh deh kohn-strook-S'YOHN eh-STAH en lah s'yoo-THAD)
near . . .	**cerca de...**
	(SEHR-kah deh)

41

far away from . . .	**lejos de...**
	(LEH-hohs deh)
at . . .	**en**
	(en)
a small town	**un pueblo**
	(oon PWEH-bloh)
the country	**el campo**
	(el KAHM-poh)
the suburbs	**las afueras de la ciudad**
	(lahs ah-FWEH-rahs de lah-s'yoo-THAD)
a shopping center	**un centro comercial**
	(oon SEN-troh koh-mehr-S'YAHL)

Establishing Priorities

The following phrases will help you tell your employees what is important to you and to the job. Note that you insert **No** to say that something is *not* necessary or important.

This is necessary.	**Esto es necesario.**
	(EH-stoh ess neh-seh-SAHR-yoh)
This is not necessary.	**Esto no es necesario.**
	(EH-stoh NOH ess neh-seh-SAHR-yoh)
vital	**imprescindible**
	(eem-preh-seen-DEE-bleh)
important	**importante**
	(eem-por-TAHN-teh)
the most important	**lo más importante**
	(loh MAHS eem-por-TAHN-teh)

urgent	**urgente**
	(oor-HEN-teh)
standard priority	**de prioridad normal**
	(deh pree-or-ee-THAD nor-MAHL)
low priority	**de prioridad baja**
	(deh pree-or-ee-THAD BAH-hah)

Indicating Order and Repetition of Tasks

When do you want something done? And in what order? Use the following phases to explain—and don't forget the all-important **por favor** and **gracias**.

Do this <u>first</u>.	**Haga esto <u>primero</u>.**
	(AH-gah EH-stoh pree-MEH-roh)
after that	**luego**
	(L'WEH-goh)
at the same time	**al mismo tiempo**
	(ahl MEEZ-moh T'YEM-poh)
beforehand	**antes**
	(AHN-tess)
afterward	**después**
	(dess-P'WESS)
soon	**pronto**
	(PROHN-toh)
right away	**en seguida**
	(en seh-GHEE-thah)
	ahora mismo
	(ah-OR-ah MEEZ-moh)

now	**ahora**
	(ah-OR-ah)
later	**más tarde / después**
	(MAHS TAHR-theh /
	dess-P'WESS)
next week	**la próxima semana**
	(lah PROHK-see-mah
	seh-MAH-nah)
at the end	**al final**
	(al fee-NAHL)

You may want something done only once, or perhaps more than once.

Do this <u>one time</u>.	**Haga esto <u>una vez</u>.**
	(AH-gah EH-stoh OO-nah BESS)
two times	**dos veces**
	(DOHS BEH-sess)
several times	**varias veces**
	(BAHR-yahs BEH-sess)
whenever needed	**cuando sea necesario**
	(kwahn-doh SEH-ah
	neh-seh-SAHR-yoh)

Chapter 3

General Instructions

In this chapter you will find phrases for giving basic instructions that can be applied to a variety of circumstances. Keep in mind that an underlined word can be replaced with a more suitable word to make it apply to a specific situation.

I need the flashlight.	**Necesito la linterna.**
	(neh-seh-SEE-toh lah leen-TEHR-nah)
the tools	**las herramientas**
	(lahs ehr-rahm-YEN-tahs)
those things	**esas cosas**
	(EH-sahs KOH-sahs)
Help me.	**Ayúdeme.**
	(ah-YOO-theh-meh)
Help him.	**Ayúdelo.**
	(ah-YOO-theh-loh)
Help them.	**Ayúdelos.**
	(ah-YOO-theh-lohs)
Help us.	**Ayúdenos.**
	(ah-YOO-theh-nos)

Show me.	**Muéstreme.**
	(M'WESS-treh-meh)
Tell me.	**Dígame.**
	(DEE-gah-meh)
Give me.	**Déme.**
	(DEH-meh)
Do it like this.	**Hágalo así.**
	(AH-gah-loh ah-SEE)
Don't do it like that.	**No lo haga así.**
	(NOH loh AH-gah ah-SEE)
Leave it like that.	**Déjelo así.**
	(DEH-heh-loh ah-SEE)
Use <u>this tool</u>.	**Use esta herramienta.**
	(OO-seh EH-stah ehr-rahm-YEN-tah)
this product	**este producto**
	(EH-steh proh-THOOK-toh)
Turn it <u>clockwise</u>.	**Gírelo a la derecha.**
	(HEE-reh-loh ah lah deh-REH-chah)
counterclockwise	**a la izquierda**
	(ah lah ees-K'YEHR-thah)
Start.	**Empiece.**
	(em-P'YEH-seh)
Stop.	**Pare.**
	(PAH-reh)
Wait.	**Espere.**
	(eh-SPEH-reh)
Clean up.	**Limpie.**
	(LEEMP-yeh)
<u>Take out</u> the trash.	**Saque la basura.**
	(SAH-keh lah bah-SOO-rah)

General Instructions

Remove	**Quite**
	(KEE-teh)
Open the door.	**Abra la puerta.**
	(AH-brah lah PWEHR-tah)
Close	**Cierre**
	(S'YEHR-reh)
Turn on the water.	**Abra la llave del agua.**
	(AH-brah lah YAH-beh del AH-gwah)
Turn off	**Cierre**
	(S'YEHR-reh)
Turn on the lights.	**Encienda la luz.**
	(en-S'YEN-dah lah LOOSE)
Turn off	**Apague**
	(ah-PAH-geh)
Lock up.	**Cierre con llave.**
	(S'YEHR-reh kohn YAH-beh)

Safety Precautions

The following phrases will help you ensure the safety of your employees and others.

Danger!	**¡Peligro!**
	(peh-LEE-groh)
Be careful!	**¡Tenga cuidado!**
	(TENG-gah kwee-THAH-thoh)
Don't go there.	**No vaya ahí.**
	(NOH BAH-yah ah-EE)
over there	**allí**
	(ah-YEE)

in that area	**a esa área**
	(ah EH-sah AH-reh-ah)
in the danger zone	**a la zona peligrosa**
	(ah lah SOH-nah
	peh-lee-GROH-sah)
across the red line	**al otro lado de la línea roja**
	(ahl oh-troh lah-thoh deh lah
	LEEN-yah ROH-hah)
the yellow tape	**la cinta amarilla**
	(lah SEEN-tah ah-mah-REE-yah)
Don't touch this.	**No toque esto.**
	(NOH TOH-keh EH-stoh)
that	**eso**
	(EH-soh)

Safety Equipment

The following words refer to equipment that workers should wear for special jobs.

Wear a hard hat.	**Póngase un casco.**
	(POHNG-gah-seh oon KAH-skoh)
protective equipment	**protección personal**
	(pro-tek-S'YOHN pehr-
	soh-NAHL)
a body harness	**un arnés del cuerpo**
	(oon ahr-NESS del KWEHR-poh)
an (orange) vest	**un chaleco (anaranjado)**
	(oon chah-LEH-koh
	[ah-nah-rahn-HAH-thoh])

General Instructions

a fall arrester	**un sistema de detención de caídas**
	(oon see-STEH-mah deh deh-ten-S'YOHN deh kah-EE-thahs)
a safety belt	**un cinturón de seguridad**
	(oon seen-too-ROHN deh seh-goo-ree THAD)
a face shield	**una máscara**
	(oo-nah MAH-skah-rah)
a dust mask	**una máscara contra el polvo**
	(oo-nah MAH-skah-rah kohn-trah el POHL-voh)
a respirator	**una máscara respiradora**
	(oo-nah MAH-skah-rah reh-spee-rah-THOR-ah)
goggles	**lentes de seguridad**
	(LEN-tehs deh seh-goo-ree-THAD)
earplugs	**tapones para los oídos**
	(tah-POH-ness pah-rah lohs oh-EE-thohs)
ear protectors	**protector de oídos**
	(proh-tek-TOR deh oh-EE-thohs)
leather gloves	**guantes de cuero**
	(GWAHN-tess deh KWEH-roh)
rubber	**de goma**
	(deh GOH-mah)

knee pads	**protector de rodillas**
	(proh-tek-TOR deh
	roh-THEE-yahs)
long pants	**pantalones largos**
	(pahn-tah-LOH-ness
	LAHR-gohs)
long sleeves	**mangas largas**
	(MAHNG-gahs LAHR-gahs)
<u>leather</u> boots	**botas <u>de cuero</u>**
	(BOH-tahs deh KWEH-roh)
rubber	**de goma**
	(deh GOH-mah)
steel-toe boots	**botas con punta de hierro**
	(BOH-tahs kohn POON-tah
	deh YEHR-roh)
heavy shoes	**zapatos gruesos**
	(sah-PAH-tohs GR'WEH-sohs)
your beeper	**su beeper**
	(soo BEE-pehr)

Emergencies

The Spanish word for *emergency* looks a lot like the English word, but is pronounced very differently. It's a good word to memorize right away, because it's so important—and you won't want to take the time to look it up.

emergency	**emergencia**
	(eh-mehr-HENSE-yah)

General Instructions

In an emergency yell "help."	**En una emergencia <u>grite</u> <u>'help' / auxilio.</u>**
	(en oo-nah eh-mehr-HENSE-yah GREE-teh 'HELP' / ah'ook-SEEL-yoh)
call for the supervisor	**llame al supervisor**
	(YAH-meh ahl soo-pehr-bee-SOR)
look for me	**búsqueme**
	(BOOSE-keh-meh)
Don't move.	**No se mueva.**
	(NOH seh M'WEH-bah)
Try to calm down.	**Trate de calmarse.**
	(TRAH-teh deh kahl-MAHR-seh)
Stay with him.	**Quédese con él.**
	(KEH-theh-seh kohn EL)
Try to calm him down.	**Trate de calmarlo.**
	(TRAH-teh deh kahl-MAHR-loh)
We're giving you first aid.	**Le vamos a dar primeros auxilios.**
	(leh BAH-mohs ah dahr pree-MEH-rohs ah'ook-SEEL-yohs)
We're taking you to a doctor.	**Lo vamos a llevar a un médico.**
	(loh BAH-mohs ah yeh-BAHR ah oon MEH-thee-koh)
Please answer my questions.	**Por favor, conteste mis preguntas.**
	(por fah-BOR kohn-TESS-teh meese preh-GOON-tahs)
What happened?	**¿Qué pasó?**
	(KEH pah-SOH)
Where did it happen?	**¿Dónde fue?**
	(DOHN-deh FWEH)

Is anyone else inside?	**¿Está adentro alguien más?**
	(eh-STAH ah-THEN-troh ahl-g'yen MAHS)
Are you sick?	**¿Está enfermo?**
	(eh-STAH en-FEHR-moh)
Are you hurt?	**¿Está herido?**
	(eh-STAH eh-REE-thoh)
Where does it hurt?	**¿Dónde le duele?**
	(DOHN-deh leh DWEH-leh)

Locations of Things

The following expressions will help you tell where things are, or where they should be. Note that certain expressions end with **de**. If the word that follows is of "masculine" gender, like **camión**, **de** will change to **del**. If the word that follows is of "feminine" gender, like **casa**, **de la** is used.

It's here.	**Está aquí.**
	(eh-STAH ah-KEE)
there	**allí**
	(ah-YEE)
in front of the house	**delante de la casa**
	(deh-LAHN-teh deh lah KAH-sah)
in back of	**detrás del camión**
	(deh-TRASS del kahm-YOHN)
next to	**al lado de**
	(ahl-LAH-thoh deh)
on top of	**encima de**
	(en-SEE-mah deh)

under	**debajo de**
	(de-BAH-hoh deh)
across from	**enfrente de**
	(en-FREN-teh deh)
between the house and	**entre la casa y la calle**
the street	(EN-treh lah KAH-sah ee
	lah KAH-yeh)
inside	**adentro**
	(ah-THEN-troh)
outside	**afuera**
	(ah-FWEH-rah)
upstairs (up there)	**arriba**
	(ahr-REE-bah)
downstairs (down there)	**abajo**
	(ah-BAH-hoh)

Going Places and Taking Things

Construction work involves a lot of moving from one place to another. To tell someone to go somewhere, use the word **a** for *to*. If the place of destination begins with **la**, as in **la casa**, say **a la casa** for *to the house*. If the place begins with **el**, as in **el edificio**, make **a** and **el** into one word—**al**. *To the building* is **al edificio**.

Come here.	**Venga acá.**
	(BENG-gah ah-KAH)
Bring me the keys.	**Tráigame las llaves.**
	(TRY-gah-meh lahs YAH-bess)
Go to the house.	**Vaya a la casa.**
	(BAH-yah ah lah KAH-sah)

to the worksite	**al sitio de trabajo**
	ahl SEET-yoh deh trah-
	BAH-hoh)
Take it to the sidewalk.	**Llévelo a la acera.**
	(YEH-beh-loh ah lah ah-SEH-rah)
over there	**para allá**
	(pah-rah ah-YAH)
to the truck	**al camión**
	(ahl kahm-YOHN)
to the trailer	**al trailer**
	(ahl TRY-lehr)
to the dumpster	**al contenedor para**
	escombros
	(ahl kohn-teh-neh-THOR
	pah-rah eh-SKOHM-brohs)
to the dump	**al tiradero**
	(ahl tee-rah-THEH-roh)
to the supervisor	**al supervisor**
	(ahl soo-pehr-bee-SOR)
to the office	**al despacho**
	(ahl deh-SPAH-choh)
home with you	**a su casa**
	(ah soo KAH-sah)

To indicate where to put something, you can use **en** to mean *in*, *on*, or *at*.

Put that . . .	**Ponga eso...**
	(POHNG-gah EH-soh)

on the ground.

en el suelo.

(en el SWEH-loh)

on the truck.

en el camión.

(en el kahm-YOHN)

in the trash.

en la basura.

(en lah bah-SOO-rah)

here.

aquí.

(ah-KEE)

over there.

allí.

(ah-YEE)

in the hole.

en el hoyo.

(en el OH-yoh)

in the toolbox.

en la caja de herramientas.

(en lah KAH-hah deh ehr-rahm-
YEN-tahs)

in the toolroom.

en el cuarto de herramientas.

(en el K'WAHR-toh deh
ehr-rahm-YEN-tahs)

in your tool belt.

**en su cinturón de herra-
mientas.**

(en soo seen-too-ROHN deh
ehr-rahm-YEN-tahs)

under the tarp.

debajo de la lona.

(deh-BAH-hoh deh lah
LOH-nah)

the cover.

la cubierta.

(lah koob-YEHR-tah)

Measuring

These phrases will help you explain the importance of accurate measurements in all aspects of construction, and how to get them. The Spanish words for *measure* and *measurements* are as follows:

to measure	**medir**
	(meh-THEER)
Please measure . . .	**Mida, por favor...**
	(MEE-thah por fah-BOR)
measurements	**medidas**
	(meh-THEE-thahs)
Be precise.	**Sea preciso.**
	(SEH-ah preh-SEE-soh)
Measure twice before cutting.	**Mida dos veces antes de cortar.**
	(MEE-thah DOHS BEH-sess ahn-tess deh kor-TAHR)
Write the measurements down.	**Anote las medidas.**
	(ah-NOH-teh lahs meh-THEE-thahs)
Check the layout.	**Cheque el trazo.**
	(CHEH-keh el TRAH-soh)
the drawing	**el dibujo**
	(el dee-BOO-hoh)
Use a tape measure.	**Use una cinta métrica.**
	(OO-seh oo-nah SEEN-tah MEH-tree-kah)
a ruler	**una regla**
	(oo-nah REH-glah)
a range finder	**un telémetro**
	(oon teh-LEH-meh-troh)

a caliper

un calibrador

(oon kah-lee-brah-THOR)

a depth gauge

un indicador de profundidad

(oon een-dee-kah-THOR deh
    proh-foon-dee-THAD)

a square

una escuadra

(oo-nah eh-SKWAH-thrah)

a framing square

una escuadra para marcos

(oo-nah eh-SKWAH-thrah
    pah-rah MAHR-kohs)

a drywall T-square

**una escuadra T para el muro
    en seco**

(oo-nah eh-SKWAH-thrah TEH
    pah-rah el MOO-roh en
    SEH-koh)

a level

un nivel

(oon nee-BELL)

a laser level

un nivel laser

(oon nee-BELL LAH-sehr)

the plumb bob

el plomo

(el PLOH-moh)

the plumb line

la plomada

(lah ploh-MAH-thah)

Chapter 4

Specific Tasks for Outdoor Jobs

The following are names of outside places and common structures where work might be done or where employees may need to go to get supplies.

the highway	**la carretera**
	(lah kahr-reh-TEH-rah)
the road	**el camino**
	(el kah-MEE-noh)
the road shoulders	**el acotamiento**
	(el ah-koh-tahm-YEN-toh)
the bridge	**el puente**
	(el PWEN-teh)
the street	**la calle**
	(lah KAH-yeh)
the driveway	**la entrada a la casa**
	(lah en-TRAH-thah ah lah KAH-sah)
the sidewalk	**la acera**
	(lah ah-SEH-rah)
the lot	**la parcela**
	(lah par-SEH-lah)

the excavation site	**el sitio de excavación**
	(el SEE-tyoh deh eks-kah-bah-SYOHN)
the warehouse	**el almacén**
	(el ahl-mah-SEN)
the jobsite	**el sitio de trabajo**
	(el SEE-tyoh deh trah-BAH-hoh)
the house	**la casa**
	(lah KAH-sah)
the building	**el edificio**
	(el eh-thee-FEESE-yoh)
the office	**la oficina**
	(lah oh-fee-SEE-nah)
the apartment building	**el edificio de departamentos**
	(el eh-thee-FEESE-yoh deh
	deh-pahr-tah-MEN-tohs)
the shopping center	**el centro commercial**
	(el SEN-troh koh-mehr-SYAHL)
the hardware store	**la ferretería**
	(lah fehr-reh-teh-REE-ah)
the lumberyard	**el almacén de maderas**
	(el ahl-mah-SEN deh mah-THEH-rahs)
the dump	**el tiradero**
	(el tee-rah-THEH-roh)

Driving Work Vehicles and Heavy Equipment

Any employee who drives a work vehicle will already have had instruction and received a permit. The following phrases will help you remind drivers of safety precautions.

Be alert.	**Manténgase alerta.**
	(mahn-TENG-gah-seh ah-LEHR-tah)

Do not use . . .	**No use...**
	(NOH OO-seh)
drugs.	**drogas.**
	(DROH-gahs)
alcohol.	**alcohol.**
	(ahl-koh-OHL)
Do not smoke while driving.	**No fume mientras maneja.**
	(NOH FOO-meh myen-trahs
	mah-NEH-hah)
Use the turn signals.	**Use los indicadores de dirección.**
	(OO-seh lohs een-dee-kah-THOR-ess
	deh dee-rek-SYOHN)
In case of an accident . . .	**En caso de un accidente...**
	(en KAH-soh deh oon ahk-see-
	THEN-teh)
stop immediately.	**párese en seguida.**
	(PAH-reh-seh en seh-
	GHEE-thah)
turn off the engine.	**apague el motor.**
	(ah-PAH-geh el moh-TOR)
call for help.	**llame por ayuda.**
	(YAH-meh por ah-YOO-thah)

Vehicle Maintenance

These expressions are for the normal running and maintenance of a vehicle.

Fill up the tank.	**Llene el tanque.**
	(YEH-neh el TAHNG-keh)

Use gasoline.	**Use gasolina.**
	(OO-seh gah-soh-LEE-nah)
diesel fuel	**combustible diesel**
	(kohm-boo-STEE-bleh DEE-sell)
Check the oil.	**Cheque la cantidad de aceite.**
	(CHEH-keh lah kahn-tee-THAD deh ah-SAY-teh)
tire pressure	**la presión de las llantas**
	(lah preh-SYOHN deh lahs YAHN-tahs)
Change the oil.	**Cambie el aceite.**
	(KAHM-byeh el ah-SAY-teh)
tire	**la llanta**
	(lah YAHN-tah)
battery	**la pila**
	(lah PEE-lah)

Driving Instructions for a Work Vehicle

Go slowly.	**Vaya despacio.**
	(BAH-yah dess-PAH-syoh)
faster	**más rápido**
	(MAHS RAH-pee-thoh)
forward	**adelante**
	(ah-theh-LAHN-teh)
back	**para atrás**
	(pah-rah ah-TRAHS)
around that	**alrededor de eso**
	(ahl-reh-theh-THOR deh EH-soh)

Specific Tasks for Outdoor Jobs

Turn around.	**Dése una vuelta.**
	(DEH-seh oo-nah BWELL-tah)
Back up.	**Venga para atrás.**
	(BENG-gah pah-rah ah-TRAHS)
Come back. (Return.)	**Vuelva.**
	(BWELL-bah)
Load it.	**Cárguelo.**
	(KAHR-geh-loh)
Unload it.	**Descárguelo.**
	(dess-KAR-geh-loh)
Move it.	**Muévalo.**
	(MWEH-bah-loh)
Raise it.	**Súbalo.**
	(SOO-bah-loh)
Lower it.	**Bájelo.**
	(BAH-heh-loh)
Put it <u>upright</u>.	**Póngalo <u>derecho</u>.**
	(POHNG-gah-lo deh-REH-choh)
upside down	**al revés**
	(ahl reh-BESS)
on its side	**de un lado**
	(deh oon LAH-thoh)
Stop.	**Pare.**
	(PAH-reh)
Brake.	**Frene.**
	(FREH-neh)
Stop at the corner.	**Pare en la esquina.**
	(PAH-reh en lah eh-SKEE-nah)

Roadwork

This section deals with some typical chores for road workers. There are different words in Spanish for different types of roads.

a minor road	**un camino**
	(oon kah-MEE-noh)
a street	**una calle**
	(oo-nah KAH-yeh)
a major (in-town) road (for vehicles)	**una calle**
	(oo-nah KAH-yeh)
a major (out-of-town) road (for vehicles)	**una carretera**
	(oo-nah kahr-reh-TEH-rah)
a freeway or interstate highway	**una autopista**
	(oo-nah ahoo-toh-PEE-stah)
Put up the <u>orange cones</u>.	**Ponga <u>los conos anaranjados</u>.**
	(POHNG-gah lohs KOH-nohs ah-nah-ran-HAH-thohs)
signs	**las señales**
	(lahs sen-YAH-less)
Direct the traffic.	**Dirija el tráfico.**
	(dee-REE-hah el TRAH-fee-koh)
Repair the <u>potholes</u>.	**Repare <u>los hoyos</u>.**
	(re-PAH-reh lohs OH-yohs)
road	**la carretera**
	(lah kahr-reh-TEH-rah)
bridge	**el puente**
	(el PWEN-teh)
cracks	**las grietas**
	(lahs GRYEH-tahs)
sidewalk	**la acera**
	(lah ah-SEH-rah)

Specific Tasks for Outdoor Jobs

Fill it with rocks.	**Llénela con piedras.**
	(YEH-neh-lah kohn P'YEH-thrahs)
gravel	**grava**
	(GRAH-bah)
dirt	**tierra**
	(T'YEHR-rah)
concrete	**concreto**
	(kohn-KREH-toh)
asphalt	**asfalto**
	(ahs-FAHL-toh)
Remove the old surface.	**Quite la superficie original.**
	(KEE-teh lah soo-pehr-FEESE-yeh oh-ree-hee-NAHL)
Break up the curb.	**Rompa el borde.**
	(ROHM-pah el BOR-theh)
Resurface it.	**Póngale una superficie nueva.**
	(POHNG-gah-leh oo-nah soo-pehr-FEES-yeh NWEH-bah)
Pave the road.	**Pavimente el camino.**
	(pah-bee-MEN-teh el kah-MEE-noh)
Use tar.	**Use brea.**
	(OO-seh BREH-ah)
Paint new lines.	**Pinte las líneas nuevas.**
	(PEEN-teh lahs LEE-neh-ahs NWEH-bahs)
Use yellow paint.	**Use pintura amarilla.**
	(OO-seh peen-TOO-rah ah-mahr-REE-yah)
white	**blanca**
	(BLAHNG-kah)

Move the Jersey barriers.	**Mueva las barreras movibles de tráfico.** (M'WEH-bah lahs bahr-REH-rahs moh-BEE-bless deh TRAH-fee-koh)

Site Preparation

The following phrases are for preparing a new site for a house or subdivision.

Set up the <u>straw-bale</u> barrier.	**Monte la barrera <u>de bala de paja</u>.** (MOHN-teh lah bahr-REH-rah deh BAH-lah deh PAH-hah)
silt fence (barrier)	**para bloquear el limo** (pah-rah bloh-keh-AHR el LEE-moh)
debris fence (barrier)	**para bloquear los escombros** (pah-rah bloh-keh-AHR lohs eh-SKOHM-brohs)
Clear the <u>brush</u>.	**Saque la <u>maleza</u>.** (SAH-keh lah mah-LEH-sah)
weeds	**la hierba mala** (lah YEHR-bah MAH-lah)
trash	**la basura** (lah bah-SOO-rah)
Cut down the bushes.	**Corte los arbustos.** (KOHR-teh lohs ahr-BOO-stohs)
Do not disturb the <u>trees</u>.	**No estorbe <u>los árboles</u>.** (NOH eh-STOR-beh lohs AHR-boh-less)

Specific Tasks for Outdoor Jobs

roots	**las raíces**
	(lahs rah-EE-sess)
Tear down . . .	**Desmantele...**
	(dess-mahn-TEH-leh)
Raze . . .	**Arrase...**
	(ahr-RAH-seh)
Break up . . .	**Rompa...**
	(ROHM-pah)
Remove . . .	**Quite...**
	(KEE-teh)
Leave . . .	**Deje...**
	(DEH-heh)
the stump.	**el tocón.**
	(el toh-KOHN)
the entire structure.	**la estructura entera.**
	(lah eh-strook-TOO-rah en-TEH-rah)
the walls.	**las paredes.**
	(lahs pah-REH-thess)
this part.	**esta parte.**
	(EH-stah PAHR-teh)
that part.	**esa parte.**
	(EH-sah PAHR-teh)
Fill it.	**Llénelo.**
	(YEH-neh-loh)
Level the ground.	**Nivele la tierra.**
	(nee-BEH-leh lah-T'YEHR-rah)
Dig a ditch to drain the water.	**Excave una zanja para drenar el agua.**
	(ek-SKAH-beh oo-nah SAHN-hah pah-rah dreh-NAHR el AH-gwah)

Mix the cement and the aggregate.	**Mezcle el cemento y el conglomerado.**
	(MESS-kleh el seh-MEN-toh ee el kohn-gloh-meh-RAH-thoh)
Pour . . .	**Eche...**
	(EH-cheh)
the concrete.	**el concreto.**
	(el kohn-KREH-toh)
Shovel the <u>gravel</u>.	**Amontone <u>la grava</u>.**
	(ah-mohn-TOH-neh lah GRAH-bah)
dirt	**la tierra**
	(lah T'YEHR-rah)
sand	**la arena**
	(lah ah-REH-nah)
Install the sewer pipes.	**Instale las cañerías para la alcantarilla.**
	(een-STAH-leh lahs kahn-yeh-REE-ahs pah-rah lah ahl-kahn-tah-REE-yah)
Prepare the roadbed.	**Prepare la base para la carretera.**
	(preh-PAH-reh lah BAH-seh pah-rah lah-kahr-reh-TEH-rah)
Extend the <u>street</u>.	**Extienda <u>la calle</u>.**
	(ek-ST'YEN-dah lah KAH-yeh)
curb	**el borde**
	(el BOR-deh)
Remove the curb for the driveway.	**Quite el borde para la entrada a la casa.**
	(KEE-teh el BOR-deh pah-rah lah en-TRAH-thah ah lah KAH-sah)

Install the drainpipes for the septic tank.

Instale los sumideros para el pozo séptico.

(een-STAH-leh lohs soo-mee-THEH-rohs pah-rah el POH-soh SEP-tee-koh)

Laying the Foundation

The word for *foundation* in Spanish is **el cimiento**. Do not confuse this with **cemento**, which is the word for *cement*.

the foundation

el cimiento

(el seem-YEN-toh)

the cement

el cemento

(el seh-MEN-toh)

The following phrases will help you give instructions for laying the foundation.

Excavate for the basement.

Excave un hoyo para el sótano.

(ek-SKAH-beh oon OH-yoh pah-rah el SOH-tah-noh)

a crawl space

un sótano de poca altura

(oon SOH-tah-noh deh poh-kah ahl-TOO-rah)

Dig a hole.

Excave un hoyo.

(ek-SKAH-beh oon OH-yoh)

ditch

una zanja

(oo-nah SAHN-hah)

trench

una trinchera

(oo-nah treen-CHEH-rah)

Pile the dirt there.	**Ponga la tierra ahí.**
	(POHNG-gah lah T'YEHR-rah ah-YEE)
Put some dirt back in the hole.	**Regrese un poco de la tierra al hoyo.**
	(reh-GREH-seh oon poh-koh deh lah T'YEHR-rah ahl OH-yoh)
Push the dirt against the basement walls.	**Empuje la tierra suelta contra las paredes del sótano.**
	(em-POO-heh lah T'YEHR-rah SWELL-tah kohn-trah lahs pah-REH-thess del SOH-tah-noh)
Put up the forms.	**Monte los encofrados.**
	(MOHN-teh lohs en-koh-FRAH-thohs)
Place the rebar.	**Coloque la varilla de refuerzo.**
	(koh-LOH-keh lah bah-REE-yah deh reh-F'WEHR-soh)
Pour the footing.	**Vierta la zarpa.**
	(B'YEHR-tah lah SAHR-pah)
foundation columns	**las columnas del cimiento**
	(lahs koh-LOOM-nahs del seem-YEN-toh)
walls	**las paredes**
	(lahs pah-REH-thess)
Lay the concrete blocks.	**Coloque los bloques de concreto.**
	(koh-LOH-keh lohs BLOH-kess deh kohn-KREH-toh)

Tools and Equipment for Lot and Foundation Preparation

Use the <u>shovel</u>.

Use <u>la pala</u>.
(OO-seh lah PAH-lah)

square shovel	**la pala cuadrada** (lah PAH-lah kwahth-RAH-thah)
pick	**el pico** (el PEE-koh)
mattock	**el zapapico** (el sah-pah-PEE-koh)
hoe	**el azadón** (el ah-sah-THOHN)
posthole digger	**las poseras** (lahs poh-SEH-rahs)
power auger	**la barrena** (lah bahr-REH-nah)
crowbar	**la palanca** (lah pah-LAHNG-kah)
digging bar (spud)	**la palanca excavadora** (lah pah-LAHNG-kah ek-skah-bah-THOR-ah)
bulldozer	**la niveladora** (lah nee-bell-ah-THOR-ah)
front-end loader	**el cargador delantero** (el kahr-gah-THOR deh-lahn-TEH-roh)
backhoe	**la excavadora trasera** (lah ek-skah-bah-THOR-ah trah-SEH-rah)

pneumatic vibrator (lit.: the dancer!)	**el vibrador pneumático** (el bee-brah-THOR neh-oo-MAH-tee-koh) **la bailarina** (lah by-lah-REE-nah)
electric vibrator / compactor	**el compactador** (el kohm-pak-tah-THOR)
forklift	**el montacargas** (el mohn-tah-KAHR-gahs)
sledgehammer	**el marro** (el MAHR-roh)
wheelbarrow	**la carretilla** (lah kar-reh-TEE-yah)
trencher	**el trinchador** (el treen-chah-THOR)
tractor	**el tractor** (el trak-TOR)
trailer (of a truck)	**el remolque** (el reh-MOHL-keh)
towtruck	**la grúa** (lah GROO-ah)
truck	**el camión** (el kahm-YOHN)
dumptruck	**el camión de carga** (el kahm-YOHN deh KAR-gah) **el camión de volteo** (el kahm-YOHN deh bol-TEH-oh)
pickup truck	**la camioneta** (lah kahm-yoh-NEH-tah)

van	**la camioneta**
	(lah kahm-yoh-NEH-tah)
rock crusher	**la trituradora**
	(lah tree-too-rah-THOR-ah)
cement mixer	**la hormigonera**
	(lah or-mee-goh-NEH-rah)
conveyor	**el transportador**
	(el trahn-spor-tah-THOR)

Structure Building and Carpentry

In this section you will find phrases specific to building the framework of a house.

Cut the beams.	**Corte las vigas.**
	(KOR-teh lahs BEE-gahs)
studs	**los montantes**
	(lohs mohn-TAHN-tess)
planks	**los tablones**
	(lohs tah-BLOH-ness)
posts	**los postes**
	(lohs POH-stess)
Install the hold-downs.	**Instale las piezas de anclaje.**
	(een-STAH-leh lahs P'YEH-sahs deh
	ahn-KLAH-heh)
floor joists	**las vigas del piso**
	(lahs BEE-gahs del PEE-soh)
subfloor	**el subpiso**
	(el soob-PEE-soh)

73

deck	**la losa de desplante**
	(lah LOH-sah deh dess-PLAHN-teh)
trusses	**las cerchas de madera**
	(lahs SEHR-chahs de mah-THEH-rah)
sill (bottom) plate	**la solera inferior**
	(lah soh-LEH-rah een-fehr-YOR)
top	**superior**
	(soo-pehr-YOR)
girder	**la viga principal**
	(lah BEE-gah preen-see-PAHL)
jacks (trimmers)	**los montantes para sostener el cabezal**
	(lohs mohn-TAHN-tess pah-rah soh-steh-NEHR el kah-beh-SAHL)
Nail the 2 × 4s in place.	**Clave los dos por cuatro.**
	(KLAH-beh lohs DOHS por K'WAH-troh)
the 2 × 6s	**los dos por seis**
	(lohs DOHS por SACE)
Push the framing into position.	**Empuje el marco en su lugar.**
	(em-POO-heh el MAHR-koh en soo loo-GAHR)
Put up the walls.	**Pare las paredes.**
	(PAH-reh lahs-pah-REH-thess)
interior partitions	**las particiones interiores**
	(lahs par-teese-YOH-ness een-tehr-YOR-ess)

Specific Tasks for Outdoor Jobs

load-bearing wall **la pared de carga**
(lah pah-RED deh KAR-gah)

blocks **las trabas**
(lahs TRAH-bahs)

Install the second-floor framing. **Instale la armadura del segundo piso.**
(een-STAH-leh lah ahr-mah-THOO-rah del seh-GOON-doh PEE-soh)

stair framing **la armadura de la escalera**
(lah ahr-mah-THOO-rah deh lah eh-skah-LEH-rah)

the ceiling joist **las vigas del techo**
(lahs BEE-gahs del TEH-choh)

the horizontal bracing **los tirantes horizontales**
(lohs tee-RAHN-tess oh-ree-sohn-TAH-less)

the rafters **los cabrios**
(lohs KAH-br'yohs)

Install the window header. **Instale el cabezal de la ventana.**
(een-STAH-leh el kah-beh-SAHL deh lah ben-TAH-nah)

the door headers **los cabezales de las puertas**
(lohs kah-beh-SAH-less de lahs PWEHR-tahs)

the windows **las ventanas**
(lahs ben-TAH-nahs)

doors **las puertas**
(lahs PWEHR-tahs)

front door **la puerta principal**
(lah PWEHR-tah preen-see-PAHL)

garage door	**la puerta del garaje**
	(lah PWEHR-tah del gah-RAH-heh)
exterior sheathing	**el entablado de afuera**
	(el en-tah-BLAH-thoh deh ah-FWEH-rah)
Apply <u>tar paper</u> to the sheathing.	**Pegue <u>papel de brea</u> al entablado.**
	(PEH-geh pah-PELL de BREH-ah ahl en-tah-BLAH-thoh)
house wrap	**envoltura de material resistente al agua y al viento**
	(en-bohl-TOO-rah deh mah-tehr-YAHL reh-see-STEN-teh ahl AH-gwah ee ahl B'YEN-toh)
Attach the siding on the outside walls.	**Ponga el siding.**
	(POHNG-gah el SY-theeng)
Caulk around the windows and doors.	**Ponga la masilla alrededor de las ventanas y las puertas.**
	(POHNG-gah lah mah-SEE-yah ahl-reh-theh-THOR deh lahs ben-TAH-nahs ee lahs PWEHR-tahs)
Use foam insulation.	**Use espuma aislante.**
	(OO-seh eh-SPOO-mah eye-SLAHN-teh)
Make sure it is plumb.	**Cheque el plomo.**
	(CHEH-keh el PLOH-moh)
Nail firmly.	**Clave con firmeza.**
	(KLAH-beh kohn feer-MEH-sah)
Attach it with screws.	**Péguelo con tornillos.**
	(PEH-geh-loh kohn tor-NEE-yohs)

Tighten the screws.

Apriete los tornillos.
(ah-PR'YEH-teh lohs tor-NEE-yohs)

Loosen

Suelte
(SWELL-teh)

Tools and Supplies for Structure Building

Use glue.

Use goma.
(OO-seh GOH-mah)
pegamento
(peh-gah-MEN-toh)

staples

grapas
(GRAH-pahs)

wire

alambre
(ah-LAHM-breh)

twine

macate
(mah-KAH-teh)

tape

cinta adhesiva
(SEEN-tah ah-theh-SEE-bah)

caulking

goma para sellar
(GOH-mah pah-rah seh-YAHR)
masilla
(mah-SEE-yah)

anchor bolts

pernos de anclaje
(PEHR-nohs deh ahn-
KLAH-heh)

nails

clavos
(KLAH-bohs)

joist hangers

estribos para viguetas
(eh-STREE-bohs pah-rah
bee-GEH-tahs)

77

metal clips	**pinzas metálicas**
	(PEEN-sahs meh-TAH-lee-kahs)
screws	**tornillos**
	(tor-NEE-yohs)
nuts	**tuercas**
	(T'WEHR-kahs)
bolts	**pernos**
	(PEHR-nohs)
washers	**arandelas**
	(ah-rahn-DEH-lahs)
the saw	**la sierra**
	(lah S'YEHR-rah)
the hacksaw	**el serrucho**
	(el sehr-ROO-choh)
the hammer	**el martillo**
	(el mahr-TEE-yoh)
the claw hammer	**el martillo chivo**
	(el mahr-TEE-yoh CHEE-boh)
the framing hammer	**el martillo para marcos**
	(el mahr-TEE-yoh pah-rah MAHR-kohs)
the nail gun	**la clavadora**
	(lah klah-bah-THOR-ah)
clamps	**abrazaderas**
	(ah-brah-sah-THEH-rahs)
the sledgehammer	**el marro**
	(el MAHR-roh)
the (Phillips head) screwdriver	**el desarmador (cruz)**
	(el dess-ahr-mah-THOR [kroose])

the electric screwdriver	**el desarmador eléctrico**
	(el dess-ahr-mah-THOR eh-LEK-tree-koh)
the screw gun	**la pistola de tornillo**
	(la pee-STOH-lah deh tor-NEE-yoh)
the stapler	**la grapadora**
	(lah grah-pah-THOR-ah)
the (adjustable) wrench	**la llave (ajustable)**
	(lah YAH-beh [ah-hoos-TAH-bleh])
a utility knife	**una cuchilla para uso general**
	(oo-nah koo-CHEE-yah pah-rah OO-soh heh-neh-RAHL)
the vise	**la prensa**
	(lah PREN-sah)
	el tornillo de banco
	(el tor-NEE-yoh deh BAHNG-koh)
the sawhorse	**el burro**
	(el BOOR-roh)

Roofing

The *roof* and the *ceiling* are known in Spanish by the same word:

the roof / the ceiling	**el techo**
	(el TEH-choh)

The Spanish-style curved roof tiles are called: **tejas** (TEH-hahs)

There are several words for roofing shingles:

shingle

la tabla
(lah TAH-blah)
la hoja
(lah OH-hah)
la teja de asfalto
(lah TEH-hah deh ahs-FAHL-toh)

Repairing a Roof

The following are phrases for repairing exterior **techos**.

Remove all <u>loose</u> nails.

Quite los clavos <u>sueltos</u>.
(KEE-teh lohs KLAH-bohs SWELL-tohs)

protruding

que sobresalgan
(keh soh-breh-SAHL-gahn)

Split the warped shingles.

Corte las tablas combadas.
(KOR-teh lahs TAH-blahs kohm-
BAH-thahs)

Nail <u>the segments</u> down.

Clave los segmentos.
(KLAH-beh lohs seg-MEN-tohs)

all the shingles

todas las tablas
(TOH-thahs lahs TAH-blahs)

the loose shingles

las tablas sueltas
(lahs TAH-blahs SWELL-tahs)

Remove the rotted sheathing.

Quite el entablado podrido.
(KEE-teh el en-tah-BLAH-thoh
pohth-REE-thoh)

Attach the feathering strips.	**Pegue los listones.**
	(PEH-geh lohs lee-STOH-ness)
Sweep the surface.	**Barra el área.**
	(BAHR-rah el AH-reh-ah)
Replace the missing shingles with new ones.	**Pegue tablas nuevas donde haga falta.**
	(PEH-geh TAH-blahs N'WEH-bahs dohn-deh ah-gah FAHL-tah)
Align the new shingles with the old ones.	**Alinee las tablas nuevas con las originales.**
	(ah-lee-NEH-eh lahs TAH-blahs N'WEH-bahs kohn lahs oh-ree-hee-NAHL-ess)

Putting on a New Roof

The following phrases will help you give instructions for installing a new roof.

Nail the sheathing in place.	**Clave el entablado.**
	(KLAH-beh el en-tah-BLAH-thoh)
Install the vent.	**Instale el escape.**
	(een-STAH-leh el eh-SKAH-peh)
Cover it with a tarp.	**Cúbralo con una lona.**
	(KOO-brah-loh kohn oo-nah LOH-nah)
Cut the roofing felt.	**Corte la felpa.**
	(KOR-teh lah FELL-pah)
Attach the felt to the sheathing.	**Pegue la felpa al entablado.**
	(PEH-geh lah FELL-pah ahl en-tah-BLAH-thoh)

Strike layout lines for aligning the rows.

Dibuje líneas para alinear las filas.
(dee-BOO-heh LEEN-yahs pah-rah ah-lee-neh-AHR lahs FEE-lahs)

Nail the shingles in place.

Clave las tablas.
(KLAH-beh lahs TAH-blahs)

Lay out single rows.

Coloque las tablas en filas sencillas.
(koh-LOH-keh lahs TAH-blahs en FEE-lahs sen-SEE-yahs)

Align the rows.

Alinee las filas.
(ah-lee-NEH-eh lahs FEE-lahs)

Cut the roof flashing.

Corte el tapajuntas.
(KOR-teh el tah-pah-HOON-tahs)

Attach the flashing.

Pegue el tapajuntas.
(PEH-geh el tah-pah-HOON-tahs)

Attach the gutter.

Pegue el canal.
(PEH-geh el kah-NAHL)

Seal around the vent pipes.

Selle alrededor de los escapes.
(SEH-yeh ahl-reh-theh-THOR deh lohs eh-SKAH-pess)

attic vents

los escapes del ático
(lohs eh-SKAH-pess del AH-tee-koh)

skylights

las claraboyas
(lahs klah-rah-BOY-ahs)

Tools and Equipment for Roofing

Use a fall arrest system.

Use un sistema de detención de caídas.

(OO-seh oon see-STEH-mah deh deh-ten-S'YOHN deh kah-EE-thahs)

Wear a safety harness.

Póngase un arnés de seguridad.

(POHNG-gah-seh oon ahr-NESS-deh seh-goo-ree-THAD)

safety goggles

lentes de seguridad

(LEN-tess deh seh-goo-ree-THAD)

knee pads

protector de rodillas

(proh-tek-TOR deh roh-THEE-yahs)

a nail pouch

la bolsa para los clavos

(lah BOHL-sah pah-rah lohs KLAH-bohs)

a tool belt

el cinturón de herramientas

(el seen-too-ROHN deh ehr-rahm-YEN-tahs)

Use a ripout tool.

Use una herramienta de arrancar.

(OO-seh oo-nah ehr-rahm-YEN-tah deh ahr-rahng-KAHR)

aviation snips

tijeras de aviación

(tee-HEH-rahs deh ah-byah-S'YOHN)

tin snips

tijeras para escaño

(tee-HEH-rahs pah-rah eh-SKAHN-yoh)

83

a notcher	**un entallador**
	(oon en-tah-yah-THOR)
a caulking gun	**una selladora**
	(oo-nah seh-yah-THOR-ah)
	una pistola de caulking
	(oo-nah pee-STOH-lah deh KOHL-keeng)
a utility knife	**una cuchilla para uso general**
	(oo-nah koo-CHEE-yah pah-rah OO-soh heh-neh-RAHL)
chalk	**tiza**
	(TEE-sah)
a tape measure	**una cinta métrica**
	(oo-nah SEEN-tah MEH-tree-kah)
a stapler	**una grapadora**
	(oo-nah grah-pah-THOR-ah)
a hammer tacker	**una grapadora martillo**
	(oo-nah grah-pah-THOR-ah mahr-TEE-yoh)
a roofing nailer	**una clavadora para techos**
	(oo-nah klah-bah-THOR-ah pah-rah TEH-chohs)
roofing cement	**cemento para techos**
	(seh-MEN-toh pah-rah TEH-chohs)
roofing tar	**brea para techos**
	(BREH-ah pah-rah TEH-chohs)

a shingling hammer	**un martillo para tablas**
	(oon mahr-TEE-yoh pah-rah
	TAH-blahs)
nails	**clavos**
	(KLAH-bohs)

Finishing the Exterior Walls

The following are phrases for installing the exterior finish of a building. First, let's look at the different types of materials used for exterior walls. Note that there is a Spanish word for siding, **revestimiento**, but you may also hear the English *siding* (SY-theeng).

The exterior walls will be made of . . .	**Las paredes exteriores serán de...**
	(lahs pah-REH-thess ek-stehr-YOR-ess
	seh-RAHN deh)
brick.	**ladrillos.**
	(lahth-REE-yohs)
stone.	**piedra.**
	(P'YEH-thrah)
stucco.	**estuco.**
	(eh-STOO-koh)
wood siding.	**madera.**
	(mah-THEH-rah)
wood shingles.	**tablas de madera.**
	(TAH-blahs deh mah-THEH-rah)
aluminum siding.	**revestimiento de aluminio.**
	(reh-beh-steem-YEN-toh deh
	ah-loo-MEEN-yoh)

vinyl siding.

revestimiento de vinil.
(reh-beh-steem-YEN-toh deh
bee-NEEL)

corrugated metal.

de metal corrugado.
(deh meh-TAHL kohr-roo-
GAH-thoh)

The following phrases will explain how you want the work to be done. For difficult instructions, remember that you can always show how you want something done, and say:

Watch me.

Míreme.
(MEE-reh-meh)

Do it like this.

Hágalo así.
(AH-gah-loh ah-SEE)

Nail the sheathing to the wall frame.

**Clave el entablo a la armadura
de las paredes con clavos.**
(KLAH-beh el en-TAH-bloh ah lah
ahr-mah-THOO-rah deh lahs
pah-REH-thess kohn KLAH-bohs)

Attach the house wrap.

**Pegue la envoltura de material
resistente al agua y al viento.**
(PEH-geh lah en-bohl-TOO-rah deh
mah-tehr-YAHL reh-see-STEN-teh
ahl AH-gwah ee ahl B'YEN-toh)

foam insulation panels

los paneles de aislamiento
(lohs pah-NEH-less deh
ice-lahm-YEN-toh)

Attach the roofing felt to the sheathing.

Pegue la felpa al entablo.

(PEH-geh lah FELL-pah ahl en-TAH-bloh)

Nail the metal ties two feet apart.

Clave los tirantes metálicos a una distancia de dos pies.

(KLAH-beh lohs tee-RAHN-tess meh-TAH-lee-kohs ah oo-nah dee-STAHN-s'yah deh DOHS-P'YESS)

Erect the wall.

Construya la pared.

(kohn-STROO-yah lah pah-RED)

Leave a ¼ inch airspace between the wall and the sheathing.

Deje un espacio de aire de un cuarto de una pulgada entre la pared y el entablo.

(DEH-heh oon eh-SPAH-s'yoh deh EYE-reh deh oon K'WAHR-toh deh oo-nah pool-GAH-thah en-treh lah pah-RED ee el en-TAH-bloh)

Anchor the masonry material to the ties.

Sujete el material de albañilería a los tirantes.

(soo-HEH-teh el mah-tehr-YAHL deh ahl-bahn-yee-leh-REE-ah ah lohs tee-RAHN-tess)

Place the bricks . . .

Coloque los ladrillos...

(koh-LOH-keh lohs lahth-REE-yohs)

    stones

    las piedras

    (lahs P'YEH-thrahs)

like this.

así.

(ah-SEE)

Mix the <u>mortar</u>.

Mezcle <u>el mortero</u>.
(MESS-kleh el mohr-TEH-roh)

stucco

el estuco
(el eh-STOO-koh)

Apply the stucco over the surface.

Aplique el estuco sobre la superficie.
(ah-PLEE-keh el eh-STOO-koh soh-breh lah soo-pehr-FEESE-yeh)

Apply three coats of stucco.

Aplique tres capas de estuco.
(ah-PLEE-keh tress KAH-pahs deh eh-STOO-koh)

Let the base coat dry.

Deje que se seque la primera mano.
(DEH-heh keh seh SEH-keh lah pree-MEH-rah MAH-noh)

Spray the base coat with water.

Salpique la primera aplicación con agua.
(sahl-PEE-keh lah pree-MEH-rah ah-plee-kah-S'YOHN kohn AH-gwah)

<u>Rake</u> the surface.

<u>Rastrille</u> la superficie.
(rah-STREE-yeh lah soo-pehr-FEESE-yeh)

Smooth

Alise
(ah-LEE-seh)

Align the board with the top of the window frame.

Alinee la tabla en la parte superior del marco de la ventana.
(ah-lee-NEH-eh lah TAH-blah en lah pahr-teh soo-pehr-YOR del MAHR-koh deh lah ben-TAH-nah)

Specific Tasks for Outdoor Jobs

Make a chalk line for the bottom of the board.

Marque con tiza una línea para la parte de abajo de la tabla.

(MAHR-keh kohn TEE-sah oo-nah LEEN-yah pah-rah lah pahr-teh deh ah-BAH-hoh deh lah TAH-blah)

Nail the boards.

Clave las tablas.

(KLAH-beh lahs TAH-blahs)

Align the boards.

Alinee las tablas.

(ah-lee-NEH-eh lahs TAH-blahs)

Caulk the siding joints.

Enmasille las juntas del revestimiento.

(en-mah-SEE-yeh lahs HOON-tahs del reh-beh-steem-YEN-toh)

Use the preformed trim.

Use el molding preformado.

(OO-seh el MOHL-theeng preh-for-MAH-thoh)

Make trim pieces to fit the edges.

Haga pedazos de molding para los bordes.

(AH-gah peh-THAH-sohs deh MOHL-theeng pah-rah lohs BOR-dess)

Set up two ladders with ladder jacks.

Monte dos escaleras con gatos de escaleras.

(MOHN-teh DOHS-eh-skah-LEH-rahs kohn GAH-tohs deh eh-skah-LEH-rahs)

Set up the posts for the pump jacks.

Monte los postes para los gatos de andamio.

(MOHN-teh lohs POH-stess pah-rah lohs GAH-tohs deh ahn-DAHM-yoh)

Chapter 5

Indoor Construction Work

The following names of rooms of a house or an office building may be useful for indicating where you want particular jobs done.

the room	**el cuarto**
	(el KWAHR-toh)
the kitchen	**la cocina**
	(lah koh-SEE-nah)
the bathroom	**el baño**
	(el BAHN-yoh)
the living room	**la sala**
	(lah SAH-lah)
the dining room	**el comedor**
	(el koh-meh-THOR)
the bedroom	**el dormitorio**
	(el dor-mee-TOR-yoh)
	el cuarto
	(el KWAHR-toh)
the hall	**el pasillo**
	(el pah-SEE-yoh)

the office	**la oficina**
	(lah oh-fee-SEE-nah)
the utility room	**el lavadero**
	(el lah-bah-THEH-roh)
the basement	**el sótano**
	(el SOH-tah-noh)
the attic / loft	**el ático**
	(el AH-tee-koh)
	el desván
	(el dess-BAHN)
the porch	**el porche**
	(el POR-cheh)
the garage	**el garaje**
	(el gah-RAH-heh)
the wall	**la pared**
	(lah pah-RED)
the ceiling	**el techo**
	(el TEH-choh)
the floor	**el piso**
	(el PEE-soh)
the fireplace	**la chimenea**
	(lah chee-meh-NEH-ah)

Installing Insulation

Often a word that ends in *tion*, *sion*, or just *ion* in English has a counterpart in Spanish that ends in **ción**, **sión**, or **ión**. Making **comparaciones** with these words is a great way to build your vocabulary in Spanish. Start with **instalación**, **ventilación**, **posición**. Naturally, there are always **excepciones**—and one is the word for *insulation*:

the insulation

el aislamiento

(el ice-lahm-YEN-toh)

Before you begin . . .

Antes de empezar...

(AHN-tess deh em-peh-SAHR)

wear protection.

lleve protección.

(YEH-beh proh-tek-S'YOHN)

Caulk around the pipes.

Masille (Kokee) alrededor de
las tuberías.

(mah-SEE-yeh [koh-KEH-eh]
ahl-reh-theh-thor deh lahs
too-beh-REE-ahs)

vents

los escapes

(lohs eh-SKAH-pess)

wiring

los cables

(lohs KAH-bless)

Install the insulation in the roof.

Instale el aislamiento en el techo.

(een-STAH-leh el ice-lahm-YEN-toh
en el TEH-choh)

in the attic

en el ático

(en el AH-tee-koh)

in the walls

en las paredes

(en lahs pah-REH-thess)

in the floors

en los pisos

(en lohs PEE-sohs)

around the air ducts

alrededor de los conductos
de aire

(ahl-reh-theh-thor deh lohs
kohn-DOOK-tohs deh
EYE-reh)

around the pipes **alrededor de los tubos**
(ahl-reh-theh-thor deh lohs
TOO-bohs)

between the rafters **entre las vigas**
(en-treh lahs BEE-gahs)

To install blanket insulation . . . **Para instalar el aislamiento tipo manta...**
(pah-rah een-stah-LAHR el ice-lahm-YEN-toh TEE-poh MAHN-tah)

press the roll in place. **coloque el rollo.**
(koh-LOH-keh el ROH-yoh)

put the vapor barrier side down. **ponga abajo el lado de la barrera de vapor.**
(POHNG-gah ah-BAH-hoh el lah-thoh deh lah bahr-REH-rah deh bah-POR)

trim it, if necessary. **recórtelo, si es necesario.**
(reh-KOR-teh-loh see ess neh-seh-SAHR-yoh)

do not compress it. **no lo comprima.**
(NOH loh kohm-PREE-mah)

place the rolls end to end. **junte los rollos uno detrás del otro.**
(JOON-teh lohs ROH-yohs OO-noh deh-TRAHS del OH-troh)

overlap the edges. **traslape los bordes.**
(trahs-LAH-peh lohs BOR-thess)

do not cover. **no cubra.**
(NOH KOO-brah)

Indoor Construction Work

Leave a three-inch clearance around . . .

Deje un espacio de tres pulgadas alrededor de...

(DEH-heh oon eh-SPAH-s'yoh deh TRESS pool-GAH-thahs ahl-reh-theh-THOR deh)

the light fixtures.

las lámparas.

(lahs LAHM-pah-rahs)

the exhaust-fan housing.

la caja del ventilador de extracción.

(lah KAH-hah del ben-tee-lah-THOR deh ek-strahk-S'YOHN)

To install fiberglass insulation . . .

Para instalar el aislamiento de fibra de vidrio...

(pah-rah een-stah-LAHR el ice-lahm-YEN-toh deh FEE-brah deh BEETHE-r'yoh)

cut the insulation into sections.

corte el aislamiento en secciones.

(KOR-teh el ice-lahm-YEN-toh en seks-YOH-ness)

separate the batts.

separe las piezas del aislamiento.

(seh-PAH-reh lahs P'YEH-sahs del ice-lahm-YEN-toh)

Seal the seams with duct tape.

Pegue las junturas con cinta de pega.

(PEH-geh lahs hoon-TOO-rahs kohn SEEN-tah deh PEH-gah)

Fit the insulation <u>behind the pipes</u>.	**Coloque el aislamiento <u>detrás de las tuberías</u>.** (koh-LOH-keh el ice-lahm-YEN-toh deh-TRAHS deh lahs too-beh-REE-ahs)
behind the electrical boxes	**detrás de las cajas eléctricas** (deh-TRAHS deh lahs KAH-hahs eh-LEK-tree-kahs)
around the windows	**alrededor de las ventanas.** (ahl-reh-theh-THOR deh lahs ben-TAH-nahs)
around the doors	**alrededor de las puertas** (ahl-reh-theh-THOR deh lahs PWEHR-tahs)
Use rigid foam panel insulation.	**Use el aislamiento de paneles rígidos.** (OO-seh el ice-lahm-YEN-toh deh pah-NEH-less REE-hee-thohs)
Blow in the loose insulation between the joists.	**Sople el aislamiento suelto por entre las vigas**. (SOH-pleh el ice-lahm-YEN-toh SWELL-toh por en-treh lahs BEE-gahs)

Interior Walls and Ceilings

Here are phrases for the installation of walls and ceilings. First, look at the Spanish words for *wall* and *ceiling*.

the wall	**la pared**
	(lah pah-RED)
the ceiling	**el techo**
	(el TEH-choh)

The Framework

Mark the positioning for the <u>wall</u>.	**Marque el armazón para <u>la pared</u>.**
	(MAHR-keh el ahr-mah-SOHN pah-rah lah pah-RED)
doorway	**el marco de la puerta**
	(el MAHR-koh deh lah PWEHR-tah)
Nail the bottom (sole) plate to the floor.	**Clave la placa inferior al piso.**
	(KLAH-beh lah PLAH-kah een-fehr-YOR ahl PEE-soh)
Brace the top plate against the ceiling.	**Pegue la placa superior al techo con un tirante.**
	(PEH-geh lah PLAH-kah soo-pehr-YOR al TEH-choh kohn oon tee-RAHN-teh)
Nail the top plate into the joists above.	**Clave la placa a las vigas de arriba.**
	(KLAH-beh lah PLAH-kah ah lahs BEE-gahs deh ahr-REE-bah)
Nail the end studs to the walls.	**Clave los montantes a las paredes.**
	(KLAH-beh lohs mohn-TAHN-tess ah lahs pah-REH-thess)

Space the wall studs <u>sixteen</u> inches apart.	**Clave los montantes a una distancia de <u>dieciséis</u> pulgadas.**
	(KLAH-beh lohs mohn-TAHN-tess ah oo-nah dee-STAHN-s'yah deh d'yeh-see-SACE pool-GAH-thahs)
twenty-four	**veinticuatro**
	(bayn-tee-KWAH-troh)
Use metal studs.	**Use montantes de metal.**
	(OO-seh mohn-TAHN-tess deh meh-TAHL)
Attach the studs with metal screws.	**Pegue los montantes con tornillos de metal.**
	(PEH-geh lohs mohn-TAHN-tess kohn tor-NEE-yohs deh meh-TAHL)
Nail the door studs to the plates.	**Clave los montantes de las puertas a las placas.**
	(KLAH-beh lohs mohn-TAHN-tess deh lahs PWEHR-tahs ah lahs PLAH-kahs)
Nail the header in place through the studs.	**Clave el cabezal de la puerta por los montantes.**
	(KLAH-beh el kah-beh-SAHL deh lah PWEHR-tah por lohs mon-TAHN-tess)
Install short (cripple) studs above the header.	**Instale montantes cortos encima del cabezal.**
	(een-STAH-leh mohn-TAHN-tess KOR-tohs en-SEE-mah del kah-beh-SAHL)

Install horizontal blocking between the studs.

Instale bloques horizontales entre los montantes.

(een-STAH-leh BLOH-kess or-ee-sohn-TAH-less en-treh lohs mohn-TAHN-tess)

Installing Drywall

The Spanish words for *drywall* are:

drywall (wallboard)	**muro en seco** (MOO-roh en SEH-koh) **tablón de yeso** (tah-BLOHN deh YEH-soh) **drywall** (DRY-wohl)
a "sheet" (of drywall)	**una hoja (de muro en seco)** (oo-nah OH-hah [deh MOO-roh en SEH-koh])
a drywall "board"	**una plancha** (oo-nah PLAHN-chah)
<u>water-resistant</u> drywall	**muro en seco <u>resistente al agua</u>** (MOO-roh en SEH-koh reh-see-STEN-teh ahl AH-gwah)
mildew-resistant	**resistente al moho** (reh-see-STEN-teh ahl MOH-oh)
fire-rated	**calificado para el fuego** (kah-lee-fee-KAH-thoh pah-rah el FWEH-goh)

Fasten the drywall <u>vertically</u>.	**Pegue el muro en seco <u>verticalmente</u>.**
	(PEH-geh el MOO-roh en SEH-koh behr-tee-kahl-MEN-teh)
horizontally	**horizontalmente**
	(or-ee-SOHN-tahl-MEN-teh)
Start at <u>the doorway</u>.	**Empiece en <u>el portal</u>.**
	(em-P'YEH-seh en el por-TAHL)
the corner	**el rincón**
	(el reeng-KOHN)
Cut holes for the <u>electrical boxes</u>.	**Corte hoyos para <u>las cajas eléctricas</u>.**
	(KOR-teh OH-yohs pah-rah las KAH-hahs eh-LEK-tree-kahs)
HVAC registers	**los registros de la calefacción y el aire acondicionado**
	(lohs reh-HEE-strohs deh lah kah-leh-fak-S'YOHN ee el eye-reh ah-kohn-dee-s'yoh-NAH-thoh)
Fasten the drywall sheet to the studs.	**Pegue la hoja de muro en seco a los montantes.**
	(PEH-geh lah OH-hah deh MOO-roh en SEH-koh a lohs mohn-TAHN-tess)
Nail from the center to the edge.	**Clave del centro hacia el borde.**
	(KLAH-beh del SEN-troh ah-s'yah el BOR-deh)

Place the nails <u>eight</u> inches apart.

Coloque los clavos a una distancia de <u>ocho</u> pulgadas.

(koh-LOH-keh lohs KLAH-bohs a oo-nah dee-STAHN-s'yah deh OH-choh pool-GAH-thahs)

twelve

doce

(DOH-seh)

Apply adhesive to the studs.

Aplique pegamento a los montantes.

(ah-PLEE-keh peh-gah-MEN-toh ah lohs mohn-TAHN-tess)

Stagger the joints.

Alterne las juntas.

(ahl-TEHR-neh lahs HOON-tahs)

Overlap the boards at the corner.

Traslape las planchas en el rincón.

(trahs-LAH-peh lahs PLAHN-chahs en el reeng-KOHN)

Scribe the board to fit at the corner.

Corte la plancha para que quepa en el rincón.

(KOR-teh lah PLAHN-chah pah-rah keh KEH-pah en el reeng-KOHN)

Attach the corner bead.

Pegue el protector de esquinas.

(PEH-geh el proh-tek-TOR deh eh-SKEE-nahs)

Cover the <u>screws</u> with joint compound.

Cubra los <u>tornillos</u> con masilla.

(KOO-brah lohs tor-NEE-yohs kohn mah-SEE-yah)

nails

los clavos

(lohs KLAH-bohs)

Let it dry.

Deje que se seque.

(DEH-heh keh seh SEH-keh)

Apply joint compound to the joints.	**Aplique masilla en las juntas.**
	(ah-PLEE-keh mah-SEE-yah en lahs HOON-tahs)
Press the joint tape into the compound.	**Apriete la cinta para juntas sobre la masilla.**
	(ah-PR'YEH-teh lah SEEN-tah pah-rah HOON-tahs soh-breh lah mah-SEE-yah)
Apply another layer of joint compound.	**Aplique otra capa de masilla sobre la cinta.**
	(ah-PLEE-keh OH-trah KAH-pah de mah-SEE-yah soh-breh lah SEEN-tah)
Sand.	**Lije.**
	(LEE-heh)

Tools for Installing Drywall

Use a <u>drywall saw</u>.	**Use un serrucho de punta.**
	(OO-seh oon sehr-ROO-choh deh POON-tah)
rasp	**una rectificadora de mano**
	(oo-nah rek-tee-fee-kah-THOR-ah deh MAH-noh)
drywall router	**una contorneadora**
	(oo-nah kohn-tor-neh-ah-THOR-ah)
drywall lift	**un gato de muro en seco**
	(oon GAH-toh deh MOO-roh en SEH-koh)

Use . . .

Use...
(OO-seh)

drywall screws.

    tornillos para muro en seco.
    (tor-NEE-yohs pah-rah MOO-roh
      en SEH-koh)

coarse-thread screws

    tornillos de rosca gruesa.
    (tor-NEE-yohs de ROH-skah
      GR'WEH-sah)

fine-thread

    de rosca fina
    (de ROH-skah FEE-nah)

Use 1¼-inch nails.

    Use clavos de una pulgada
    y cuarto.
    (OO-seh KLAH-bohs deh
      OO-nah pool-GAH-thah
      ee KWAHR-toh)

Installing Ceilings

Precut a hole for the ceiling box.

Primero, corte un hoyo para
la caja del techo.
(pree-MEH-roh KOR-teh oon OH-yoh
    pah-rah lah KAH-hah del
    TEH-choh)

ceiling register

    el escape del techo
    (el eh-SKAH-peh del TEH-choh)

Lay out a plan for the acoustic tiles.

Haga un plano para los paneles
acústicos.
(AH-gah oon PLAH-noh pah-rah
    lohs pah-NEH-less ah-KOO-
    stee-kohs)

Install the drywall on the ceiling.	**Instale el muro en seco en el techo.**
	(een-STAH-leh el MOO-roh en SEH-koh en el TEH-choh)
acoustic tiles	**los paneles acústicos**
	(lohs pah-NEH-less ah-KOO-stee-kohs)
Attach the tiles with staples.	**Pegue los paneles con grapas.**
	(PEH-geh lohs pah-NEH-less kohn GRAH-pahs)
glue	**pegamento**
	(peh-gah-MEN-toh)
Install the suspended grid.	**Instale el sistema de rejas.**
	(een-STAH-leh el see-STEH-mah de REH-hahs)
Lay in the tiles.	**Coloque los paneles.**
	(koh-LOH-keh lohs pah-NEH-less)
Start in the corner.	**Empiece en el rincón.**
	(em-P'YEH-seh en el reeng-KOHN)
center	**en el centro**
	(en el SEN-troh)

Installing Wood Moldings

Here are the names of different moldings. (You may also hear *molding* referred to as **el molding**).

baseboard molding	**la moldura del zócalo**
	(lah mohl-THOO-rah del SOH-kah-loh)

Indoor Construction Work

chair rail	**para las sillas**
	(pah-rah lahs SEE-yahs)
picture rail	**para los cuadros**
	(pah-rah lohs KWAHTH-rohs)
crown (cornice)	**para la cornisa**
	(pah-rah lah kor-NEE-sah)
casing	**del marco de la ventana /**
	la puerta
	(del mahr-koh deh lah ben-
	TAH-nah / lah PWEHR-tah)

Here are phrases for the basic installation of moldings.

Measure and cut the moldings.	**Mida y corte las molduras.**
	(MEE-thah ee KOR-teh lahs
	mohl-THOO-rahs)
Miter the ends of the outside corners.	**Sesgue las esquinas.**
	(SESS-geh lahs eh-SKEE-nahs)
Cope the joints at the inside corners.	**Remate con albardilla los rincones.**
	(reh-MAH-teh kohn ahl-bahr-THEE-
	yah lohs reeng-KOH-ness)
Use a miter box.	**Use la caja de ángulos.**
	(OO-seh lah KAH-hah deh
	AHNG-goo-lohs)
the power miter saw	**la sierra de retroceso para**
	ingletes
	(lah S'YEHR-rah deh reh-troh-
	SEH-soh pah-rah eeng-
	LEH-tess)

the coping saw	**la sierra de marquetería**
	(lah S'YEHR-rah deh mahr-keh-teh-REE-ah)
Install the molding.	**Instale las molduras.**
	(een-STAH-leh lahs mohl-THOO-rahs)
Use <u>nails</u>.	**Use <u>clavos</u>.**
	(OO-seh KLAH-bohs)
anchors	**anclajes**
	(ahng-KLAH-hess)
plastic anchors	**anclajes de plástico**
	(ahng-KLAH-hess deh PLAH-stee-koh)
panel adhesive	**pegamento para paneles**
	(peh-gah-MEN-toh pah-rah pah-NEH-less)

Windows and Doors

This section provides phrases for giving instructions for installing windows and doors. Here are the Spanish words for *window* and *door*:

window	**la ventana**
	(lah ben-TAH-nah)
door	**la puerta**
	(lah PWEHR-tah)

Types of Windows

picture window	**un ventanal**
	(oon ben-tah-NAHL)

paned window

una ventana de vidrios marcados
(oo-nah ben-TAH-nah deh BEETHE-
r'yohs mahr-KAH-thohs)

casement

con bisagras
(kohn bee-SAH-grahs)

double-hung

de doble vía
(deh DOH-bleh BEE-ah)

pivot (jalousie)

de pivote
(deh pee-BOH-teh)

pre-hung

pre-colgada
(preh-kohl-GAH-thah)

storm

contraventana
(kohn-trah-ben-TAH-nah)

de tormenta
(deh tor-MEN-tah)

screen

de tela metálica
(deh TEH-lah meh-TAH-
lee-kah)

fixed

fija
(FEE-hah)

Window Installation

Here are phrases for the basic steps in window installation.

Measure the opening.

Mida la abertura.
(MEE-thah lah ah-behr-TOO-rah)

Seal around the opening.

Selle alrededor de la abertura.
(SEH-yeh ahl-reh-theh-THOR deh lah
ah-behr-TOO-rah)

107

Center the window in the opening.

Ponga la ventana en el centro de la abertura.

(POHNG-gah lah ven-TAH-nah en el SEN-troh de lah ah-behr-TOO-rah)

Make sure the window is plumb.

Cheque que la ventana esté a plomo.

(CHEH-keh keh lah ben-TAH-nah eh-STEH ah PLOH-moh)

Nail the window into the frame.

Clave la ventana al marco.

(KLAH-beh lah ben-TAH-nah ahl MAHR-koh)

Start here.

Empiece aquí.

(em-P'YEH-seh ah-KEE)

Insert shims.

Inserte cuñas.

(een-SEHR-teh KOON-yahs)

Fill the gaps with foam.

Llene los espacios con espuma.

(YEH-neh lohs eh-SPAH-s'yohs kohn eh-SPOO-mah)

Fill the nail holes.

Rellene los hoyos de los clavos.

(reh-YEH-neh lohs OH-yohs deh lohs KLAH-bohs)

Caulk around the window.

Masille alrededor de la ventana.

(mah-SEE-yeh ahl-reh-theh-THOR deh lah ven-TAH-nah)

Types of Doors

the interior door

la puerta interior

(lah PWEHR-tah een-tehr-YOR)

exterior	**exterior**
	(ek-stehr-YOR)
sliding	**corrediza**
	(kohr-reh-THEE-sah)
folding	**plegadiza**
	(pleh-gah-THEE-sah)
panel	**de paneles**
	(deh pah-NEH-less)
flush	**lisa**
	(LEE-sah)
pre-hung	**pre-colgada**
	(preh-kohl-GAH-thah)
storm	**para tormentas**
	(pah-rah tor-MEN-tahs)
screen	**de tela metálica**
	(deh TEH-lah meh-TAH-lee-kah)
fire-resistant	**resistente al fuego**
	(reh-see-STEN-teh ahl F'WEH-goh)
garage	**del garaje**
	(del gah-RAH-heh)

Installing a Standard Door

Install the frame.	**Instale el marco.**
	(een-STAH-leh el MAHR-koh)
Make sure it is plumb.	**Cheque que esté a plomo.**
	(CHEH-keh keh eh-STEH ah PLOH-moh)

Use shims between the frame and the studs.	**Ponga cuñas entre el marco y los montantes.**
	(POHNG-gah KOON-yahs en-treh el MAHR-koh ee lohs mohn-TAHN-tess)
Trim the door if it doesn't fit.	**Recorte la puerta si no cabe.**
	(reh-KOR-teh lah PWEHR-tah see NOH KAH-beh)
Work from each corner to the center.	**Trabaje desde los rincones hacia el centro.**
	(trah-BAH-heh dez-deh lohs reeng-KOH-ness ah-s'yah el SEN-troh)
Place the door in the frame.	**Coloque la puerta en el marco.**
	(koh-LOH-keh lah PWEHR-tah en el MAHR-koh)
Install the hinges.	**Instale las bisagras.**
	(een-STAH-leh lahs bee-SAH-grahs)
Use the chisel.	**Use el cincel.**
	(OO-seh el seen-SELL)
the router	**la contorneadora**
	(lah kohn-tor-neh-ah-THOR-ah)
Install the threshhold.	**Instale el umbral.**
	(een-STAH-leh el oom-BRAHL)

Installing Sliding and Folding Doors

Screw the hanger brackets to the top of the door.	**Atornille las ménsulas a la parte superior de la puerta.**
	(ah-tor-NEE-yeh lahs MEN-soo-lahs a lah pahr-teh soo-pehr-YOR deh lah PWEHR-tah)

Indoor Construction Work

Make sure it is level.

Cheque que esté nivel.

(CHEH-keh keh eh-STEH nee-BELL)

Attach the hangers and rollers.

Ponga los ganchos y las rueditas.

(POHNG-gah lohs GAN-chohs ee lahs
r'weh-THEE-tahs)

Hang the door on the track.

Cuelgue la puerta en el carril.

(KWELL-geh lah PWEHR-tah en el
kahr-REEL)

Install the door guide on the floor.

Instale la guía en el piso.

(een-STAH-leh lah GHEE-ah en el
PEE-soh)

Attach the doorstops to the track.

Ponga los topes en el carril.

(POHNG-gah lohs TOH-pess en
el kahr-REEL)

Cover the track with a valence.

Cubra el carril con un bastidor.

(KOO-brah el kahr-REEL kohn oon
bah-stee-THOR)

Put the pivot hinges in the top of
the end door.

**Ponga las bisagras del pivote en
la parte superior de la puerta
del extremo.**

(POHNG-gah lahs bee-SAH-grahs del
pee-BOH-teh en lah pahr-teh
soo-pehr-YOR deh lah PWEHR-tah
del ek-STREH-moh)

bottom

inferior

(een-fehr-YOR)

Hinge the doors together.

Conecte las bisagras.

(koh-NEK-teh lahs bee-SAH-gras)

Attach the bottom pivot to the
floor.

Pegue el pivote inferior al piso.

(PEH-geh el pee-BOH-teh een-fehr-
YOR ahl PEE-soh)

Installing Door Hardware

Install the doorknob.	**Instale la manilla.**
	(een-STAH-leh lah mah-NEE-yah)
the lockset	**la cerradura**
	(lah sehr-rah-THOO-rah)
the knocker	**la aldaba**
	(lah ahl-DAH-bah)
the doorbell	**el timbre**
	(el TEEM-breh)
the doorstop	**el tope**
	(el TOH-peh)

Plumbing

This section provides words and phrases related to plumbing. Several plumbing words come from the word for *lead*—which is related to the word for *plumb line*:

lead	**el plomo**
	(el PLOH-moh)
plumb line	**la plomada**
	(lah ploh-MAH-thah)
the plumber	**el plomero**
	(el ploh-MEH-roh)
plumbing	**la plomería**
	(lah ploh-meh-REE-ah)

A modern way to refer to *plumbing* is with the following expression:

plumbing **instalaciones hidrosanitarias**
(een-stah-lah-S'YOH-ness eethe-roh-
sah-nee-TAHR-yahs)

You may want to explain to your employees the importance of codes and standards.

We have to do this according **Debemos cumplir con el código.**
to code. (deh-BEH-mohs koom-PLEER kohn
el KOH-thee-goh)

regulations **los reglamentos**
(lohs reh-glah-MEN-tohs)

The code is a law. **El código es una ley.**
(el KOH-thee-goh ess oo-nah LAY)

Plumbing Fixtures

Here are the names of the most common types of plumbing fixtures, and the expression for requesting their installation.

Install the kitchen sink. **Instale el fregadero.**
(een-STAH-leh el freh-gah-THEH-roh)

bathroom sink **el lavabo**
(el lah-BAH-boh)

garbage disposer **el triturador**
(el tree-too-rah-THOR)

dishwasher **el lavaplatos**
(el lah-bah-PLAH-tohs)

bathtub **la bañera**
(lah bahn-YEH-rah)

whirlpool bath	**el Jacuzzi**
	(el yah-KOO-see)
shower	**la ducha**
	(lah DOO-chah)
toilet	**el inodoro**
	(el ee-noh-THOR-oh)
bidet	**el bidé**
	(el bee-THEH)
washing machine	**la lavadora**
	(lah lah-bah-THOR-ah)
indoor faucets	**las llaves del agua**
	(lahs YAH-bess del AH-gwah)
shower control	**la llave de la ducha**
	(lah YAH-beh deh lah DOO-chah)
showerhead	**la regadera**
	(lah reh-gah-THEH-rah)
floor drain	**el desagüe del piso**
	(el dess-AH-gweh del PEE-soh)
stopper	**el tapón**
	(el tah-POHN)
cleanout	**el registro**
	(el reh-HEE-stroh)
hot-water heater	**el calentador del agua**
	(el kah-len-tah-THOR del AH-gwah)
sump pump	**la bomba de sumidero**
	(lah BOHM-bah deh soo-mee-THEH-roh)

hot tub	**la tina de remolino**
	(lah TEE-nah deh reh-moh-LEE-noh)
outdoor faucets	**las llaves de afuera**
	(lahs YAH-bess deh ah-FWEH-rah)
sill cock	**el grifo de manguera**
	(el GREE-foh deh mahn-GEH-rah)

Plumbing Installation

Install a septic system.	**Instale un sistema séptico.**
	(een-STAH-leh oon see-STEH-mah SEP-tee-koh)
Connect to the public sewer system.	**Conecte a la alcantarilla pública.**
	(koh-NEK-teh ah lah ahl-kahn-tah-REE-yah POO-blee-kah)
Connect to the pipe.	**Conecte a la tubería.**
	(koh-NEK-teh ah lah too-beh-REE-ah)
to the drainpipe	**a los tubos de drenaje**
	(ah lohs TOO-bohs deh dreh-NAH-heh)
to the sewer / storm drain	**a la alcantarilla**
	(ah lah ahl-kahn-tah-REE-yah)
Install the soil pipe.	**Instale el tubo de residuos cloacales.**
	(een-STAH-leh el TOO-boh deh reh-SEETHE-wohs kloh-ah-KAH-less)

soil stack	**el bajante**
	(el bah-HAHN-teh)
main drain	**el desagüe principal**
	(el dess-AH-gweh preen-see-PAHL)
trap	**la trampa**
	(lah TRAHM-pah)
vent line	**el respiradero**
	(el reh-spee-rah-THEH-roh)
shutoff valve	**la válvula de cierre**
	(lah BAHL-boo-lah deh S'YEHR-reh)
gas line	**la línea del gas**
	(lah LEE-neh-ah del GAHS)
Check the cold-water supply	**Cheque el suministro de agua fría.**
	(CHEH-keh el soo-mee-NEE-stroh deh AH-gwah FREE-ah)
Turn on the main valve.	**Abra la válvula principal del agua.**
	(Ah-brah lah VAHL-boo-lah preen-see-PAHL del AH-gwah)
Turn off	**Cierre**
	(S'YEHR-reh)
Drain the system.	**Vacíe el sistema.**
	(bah-SEE-eh el see-STEH-mah)
Cut the pipe.	**Corte el tubo.**
	(KOR-teh el TOO-boh)
Bend	**Doble**
	(DOH-bleh)

Cut threads on the pipe ends.

Corte roscas en los extremos de los tubos.

(KOR-teh ROHS-kahs en lohs ek-STREH-mohs deh lohs TOO-bohs)

Flare the ends of the pipe.

Abocine los extremos del tubo.

(ah-boh-SEE-neh lohs ek-STREH-mohs del TOO-boh)

Hold the pipe securely.

Sostenga bien el tubo.

(soh-STENG-gah B'YEN el TOO-boh)

Cement the pipes.

Aplique cemento a los tubos.

(ah-PLEE-keh seh-MEN-toh ah lohs TOO-bohs)

Connect the fittings.

Conecte los accesorios.

(koh-NEK-teh lohs ahk-seh-SOR-yohs)

Assemble

Arme

(AHR-meh)

Tighten . . .

Apriete...

(ah-PR'YEH-teh)

Loosen . . .

Suelte...

(SWELL-teh)

Remove the burrs from the pipe.

Quite las rebabas del tubo.

(KEE-teh lahs reh-BAH-bahs del TOO-boh)

Repair the leak.

Repare la fuga.

(reh-PAH-reh lah FOO-gah)

Unclog the toilet.

Quite la obstrucción del inodoro.

(KEE-teh lah ob-strook-S'YOHN del ee-noh-THOR-oh)

drains

desagüe

(dess-AH-gweh)

Plumbing Tools and Supplies

There are so many sizes and shapes of plumbing supplies that you might find it easier to say *Use this*. To change *use* to *don't use*, just add **No** at the beginning:

(Don't) Use this.	**(No) Use esto.**
	([NOH] OO-seh EH-stoh)
that	**eso**
	(EH-soh)
this tool	**esta herramienta**
	(EH-stah ehr-rahm-YEN-tah)
that	**esa**
	(EH-sah)
Use galvanized steel pipes.	**Use tuberías galvanizadas.**
	(OO-seh too-beh-REE-ahs gahl-bah-nee-SAH-thahs)
copper	**de cobre**
	(deh KOH-breh)
PVC	**de PVC**
	(deh PEH-BEH-SEH)
ABS	**de ABS**
	(deh AH-BEH-EH-seh)
large-diameter pipe	**tubería grande**
	(too-beh-REE-ah GRAHN-deh)
small-diameter	**pequeña**
	(peh-KEN-yah)
threaded	**con rosca**
	(kohn ROHS-kah)

a 45-degree elbow connection	**un conector de codo de 45 grados**
	(oon koh-nek-TOR deh KOH-thoh deh kwah-ren-tah ee SEENG-koh GRAH-thohs)
90-degree	**de 90 grados**
	(deh noh-BEN-tah GRAH-thohs)
Use a tee fitting.	**Use un tubo en T.**
	(OO-seh oon TOO-boh en TEH)
Y	**en Y**
	(en EE-GR'YEH-gah)
coupling	**cople**
	(KOH-pleh)
union	**unión**
	(oon-YOHN)
cap	**tapa**
	(TAH-pah)
plug	**de rosca**
	(deh ROH-skah)
Use a bushing.	**Use un anillo de reducción.**
	(OO-seh oon ah-NEE-yoh deh reh-thook-S'YOHN)
reducer	**un reductor**
	(oon reh-thook-TOR)
toilet flange	**la palanca del inodoro**
	(lah pah-LAHNG-kah del ee-noh-THOR-oh)
rubber adapter	**un adaptador de goma**
	(oon ah-thahp-tah-THOR deh GOH-mah)

trap adapter	**un adaptador de trampas**
	(oon ah-thahp-tah-THOR deh-TRAHM-pahs)
drain valve	**una válvula para drenar**
	(oo-nah BAHL-boo-lah pah-rah dreh-NAHR)
a <u>shutoff</u> valve	**una válvula <u>de cierre</u>**
	(oo-nah BAHL-boo-lah deh S'YEHR-reh)
ball	**de bola**
	(deh BOH-lah)
antisiphon	**de antisifón**
	(deh ahn-tee-see-FOHN)
a <u>single</u> control valve	**una válvula de control <u>sencillo</u>**
	(oo-nah BAHL-boo-lah deh kohn-TROHL sen-SEE-yoh)
multiple	**múltiple**
	(MOOL-tee-pleh)
a vacuum breaker	**un interruptor de vacío**
	(oon een-tehr-roop-TOR deh bah-SEE-oh)
a pipe hanger	**un gancho para tubos**
	(oon GAHN-choh pah-rah TOO-bohs)
Use an <u>adjustable</u> wrench.	**Use una llave <u>inglesa</u>.**
	(OO-seh oo-nah YAH-beh eeng-GLEH-sah)
a pipe	**de tubo**
	(deh TOO-boh)
a crescent	**de tuercas**
	(deh TWEHR-kahs)

a basin	**pico de ganso**
	(PEE-koh deh GAHN-soh)
Use <u>pliers</u>.	**Use <u>alicates</u>.**
	(OO-seh ah-lee-KAH-tess)
a file	**una lima**
	(oo-nah LEE-mah)
a plunger	**una sopapa**
	(oo-nah soh-PAH-pah)
a drain auger	**una barrena**
	(oo-nah bahr-REH-nah)
a snake	**una serpiente**
	(oo-nah sehr-P'YEN-teh)
a propane torch	**una antorcha de propano**
	(oo-nah ahn-TOR-chah deh proh-PAH-noh)
a welder	**un soldador**
	(oon sohl-thah-THOR)
a welding rod	**una barra de soldar**
	(oo-nah BAHR-rah deh sohl-DAHR)
flux	**fundete**
	(foon-DEH-teh)
a brush	**un cepillo**
	(oon seh-PEE-yoh)
a miter saw	**una sierra de retroceso**
	(oo-nah S'YEHR-rah de reh-troh-SEH-soh)
a rubber washer	**una arandela de goma**
	(oo-nah ah-rahn-DEH-lah deh GOH-mah)

a clamp	**una abrazadera**
	(oo-nah ah-brah-sah-THEH-rah)
an epoxy patch	**resina epoxídica**
	(reh-SEE-nah eh-pohk-SEE-thee-kah)
plumber's putty	**masilla para plomeros**
	(mah-SEE-yah pah-rah ploh-MEH-rohs)
pipe joint compound	**compuesto para tubos**
	(kohm-PWEH-stoh pah-rah TOO-bohs)
teflon tape	**cinta de teflon**
	(SEEN-tah deh TEF-lohng)

Tile Work

In Spanish there are special words for the different types of tiles:

roof tiles	**tejas / tablas**
	(TEH-hahs / TAH-blahs)
sidewalk tiles	**baldosas**
	(bahl-DOH-sahs)
floor tiles	**losas**
	(LOH-sahs)

Here are phrases for explaining the different steps for indoor tiling.

Indoor Construction Work

Measure the area.

Mida el área.
(MEE-thah el AH-reh-ah)

Mark the layout lines.

Marque las líneas.
(MAHR-keh lahs LEE-neh-ahs)

Make sure . . .

Cheque que...
(CHEH-keh keh)

    the wall is plumb.

    la pared esté a plomo.
    (lah pah-RED eh-STEH ah
      PLOH-moh)

    the floor is square.

    el piso esté cuadrado.
    (el PEE-soh eh-STEH kwahth-
      RAH-thoh)

    level

    nivel
    (nee-BELL)

Cut these tiles in half.

Corte estos azulejos por la mitad.
(KOR-teh eh-stohs ah-soo-LEH-hohs
    por lah mee-TAHD)

Trim the tiles.

Recorte los azulejos.
(reh-KOR-teh lohs ah-soo-LEH-hohs)

Align the tiles with the walls.

Alinee las losas con las paredes.
(ah-lee-NEH-eh lahs LOH-sahs kohn
    lahs pah-REH-thess)

Begin in the center of the room.

Empiece en el centro del cuarto.
(em-P'YEH-seh en el SEN-troh del
    KWAHR-toh)

Nail a concrete board to the walls.

**Clave una tabla de concreto a
    las paredes.**
(KLAH-beh oo-nah TAH-blah deh
    kohn-KREH-toh ah lahs pah-
    REH-thess)

Score the concrete board.

Haga unos cortes en la superficie de la tabla de concreto.

(AH-gah oo-nohs KOR-tess en lah soo-pehr-FEESE-yeh deh lah TAH-blah deh kohn-KREH-toh)

Drill the holes for the pipes.

Taladre los hoyos para los tubos.

(tah-LAHTH-reh lohs OH-yohs pah-rah lohs TOO-bohs)

the wires

los alambres

(lohs ah-LAHM-bress)

Spread the mortar.

Ponga la mezcla.

(POHNG-gah lah MESS-klah)

adhesive

la adhesiva

(lah ah-theh-SEE-bah)

Place the tiles in position.

Coloque los azulejos.

(koh-LOH-keh lohs ah-soo-LEH-hohs)

Mix the grout.

Mezcle la lechada.

(MESS-kleh lah leh-CHAH-thah)

Apply the grout between the tiles.

Aplique la lechada entre los azulejos.

(ah-PLEE-keh lah leh-CHAH-thah en-treh lohs ah-soo-LEH-hohs)

Clean off the excess grout.

Limpie la lechada de sobra.

(LEEMP-yeh lah leh-CHAH-thah deh SOH-brah)

Wipe the surface of the tiles with a damp cloth.

Pase un trapo húmedo por la superficie de los azulejos.

(PAH-seh oon TRAH-poh OO-meh-thoh por lah soo-pehr-FEESE-yeh deh lohs ah-soo-LEH-hohs)

solvent

un solvente

(oon sohl-BEN-teh)

Tools and Supplies for Tile Work

Use a tile saw.

Use una sierra para azulejos.

(OO-seh oo-nah S'YEHR-rah pah-rah
ah-soo-LEH-hohs)

a tile nipper

una pinza para cortar losetas

(oo-nah PEEN-sah pah-rah
kor-TAHR loh-SEH-tahs)

a grout saw

una sierra para lechada

(oo-nah S'YEHR-rah pah-rah
leh-CHAH-thah)

a carbide hole saw

una sierra de carbudo

(oo-nah S'YEHR-rah deh
kahr-BOO-thoh)

a rubbing stone

una piedra pómez

(oo-nah P'YEH-thrah
POH-mess)

a flat trowel

una paleta plana

(oo-nah pah-LEH-tah
PLAH-nah)

notched

con muescas

(kohn M'WESS-kahs)

a grout float

una flota de calidad

(oo-nah FLOH-tah deh kah-
lee-THAD)

a rubber mallet

un mazo de goma

(oon MAH-soh deh GOH-mah)

cheesecloth	**bambula**
	(bahm-BOO-lah)
a sponge	**una esponja**
	(oo-nah eh-SPOHN-hah)
Wear <u>knee pads</u>.	**Lleve <u>protector de rodillas</u>.**
	(YEH-beh proh-tek-TOR deh
	roh-THEE-yahs)
goggles	**lentes de seguridad**
	(LEN-tess deh seh-goo-ree-
	THAD)
a dust mask	**una mascarilla para el polvo**
	(oo-nah mah-skah-REE-yah
	pah-rah el POHL-boh)

Electrical Wiring and Installation

First, let's look at the Spanish word for *electricity*:

electricity	**la electricidad**
	(lah eh-lek-tree-see-THAD)

You can learn many new Spanish words by substituting **idad** for *ity* in some English words, as in **posibilidad**, **oportunidad**. Here are phrases for working with **la electricidad**.

We have to do this according to code.	**Debemos cumplir con el código.**
	(deh-BEH-mohs koom-PLEER kohn
	el KOH-thee-goh)

Be sure to follow the safety regulations.

Asegúrese de seguir los reglamentos de seguridad.

(ah-seh-GOO-reh-seh deh seh-GEER lohs reh-glah-MEN-tohs deh seh-goo-ree-THAD)

Electrical Projects

Install the breaker panel.

Instale el panel de los interruptores automáticos.

(een-STAH-leh el pah-NELL de lohs een-tehr-roop-TOR-ess ah'oo-toh-MAH-tee-kohs)

breaker

el interruptor automático

(el een-tehr-roop-TOR ah'oo-toh-MAH-tee-koh)

Connect the circuits.

Conecte los circuitos.

(koh-NEK-teh lohs seer-KWEE-tohs)

electrical boxes

las cajas eléctricas

(lahs KAH-hahs eh-LEK-tree-kahs)

Install the receptacles.

Instale los enchufes.

(een-STAH-leh lohs en-CHOO-fehs)

GFI receptacle

el enchufe GFI

(el en-CHOO-feh HEH-EH-feh-EE)

240 volt outlet

el enchufe de 240 voltios

(el en-CHOO-feh deh dohs-S'YEN-tohs kwah-REN-tah BOHL-t'yohs)

telephone jacks	**los enchufes de teléfono**
	(lohs en-CHOO-fess deh
	teh-LEH-foh-noh)
cable TV jacks	**los enchufes para la antena**
	(lohs en-choo-fess pah-rah lah
	ahn-TEH-nah)
<u>bathroom</u> fan	**el ventilador <u>del baño</u>**
	(el ben-tee-lah-THOR del
	BAHN-yoh)
ceiling	**del techo**
	(del TEH-choh)
attic	**del ático**
	(del AH-tee-koh)
the smoke alarm	**la alarma contra fuego**
	(lah ah-LAHR-mah kohn-trah
	FWEH-goh)
doorbell	**el timbre**
	(el TEEM-breh)
garage-door opener	**el abridor de garaje**
	(el ah-bree-THOR deh
	gah-RAH-heh)
a backup generator	**un generador de emergencia**
	(oon heh-neh-rah-THOR deh
	eh-mehr-HEN-s'yah)

Lighting Projects

Install . . .

Instale...

(een-STAH-leh)

the <u>single-pole</u> switch.

el interruptor <u>de una vía</u>.

(el een-tehr-roop-TOR deh
OO-nah BEE-ah)

three-way

de tres vías

(deh TRESS BEE-ahs)

dimmer

el regulador de luz

(el reh-goo-lah-THOR deh
LOOSE)

ceiling fixtures

los ornamentos del techo

(lohs or-nah-MEN-tohs del
TEH-choh)

recessed light fixtures

las luces recesadas

(lahs LOO-sess reh-seh-
SAH-thahs)

flourescent fixtures

las luces fluorescentes

(lahs LOO-sess floo'oh-reh-
SEN-tess)

track lights

las luces de riel

(lahs LOO-sess deh R'YELL)

floodlight

el reflector de haz difuso

(el reh-flek-TOR deh AHS
dee-FOO-soh)

outdoor lighting

las luces de afuera

(lahs LOO-sess deh ah-
FWEH-rah)

Electrical Appliances

Connect the <u>appliances</u>.	**Conecte <u>los electrodomésticos</u>.**
	(koh-NEK-teh lohs eh-lek-troh-thoh-MEH-stee-kohs)
stove	**la estufa**
	(lah eh-STOO-fah)
refrigerator	**la nevera**
	(lah neh-BEH-rah)
	el refrigerador
	(el reh-free-heh-rah-THOR)
dishwasher	**el lavaplatos**
	(el lah-bah-PLAH-tohs)
washing machine	**la lavadora**
	(lah lah-bah-THOR-ah)
dryer	**la secadora**
	(lah seh-kah-THOR-ah)

General Instructions for Electrical Installation

<u>Turn off</u> the electricity.	**<u>Apague</u> la electricidad.**
	(ah-PAH-geh lah eh-lek-tree-see-THAD)
Turn on	**Encienda**
	(en-S'YEN-dah)
Flip the circuit breaker.	**Prenda el interruptor automático.**
	(PREN-dah el een-tehr-roop-TOR ah'oo-toh-MAH-tee-koh)
Drill through <u>the studs</u>.	**Atornille por <u>los montantes</u>.**
	(ah-tor-NEE-yeh por lohs mohn-TAHN-tess)

Indoor Construction Work

the <u>ceiling</u> joists

las vigas del techo
(lahs BEE-gahs del TEH-choh)

floor

del piso
(del PEE-soh)

Pull the cable through the <u>ceiling</u>.

Jale el cable por <u>el techo</u>.
(HAH-leh el KAH-bleh por el TEH-choh)

attic

el ático
(el AH-tee-koh)

wall

la pared
(lah pah-RED)

Do not staple the cable across the joist.

No engrape el cable por las vigas.
(NOH en-GRAH-peh el KAH-bleh por lahs BEE-gahs)

Ground the <u>system</u>.

Ponga tierra <u>al sistema</u>.
(POHNG-gah T'YEHR-rah ahl see-STEH-mah)

individual circuits

a los circuitos individuales
(ah lohs seer-KWEE-tohs een-dee-bee-TH'WAH-less)

Make sure all the receptacles are grounded.

Cheque que los receptáculos estén conectados a tierra.
(CHEH-keh keh lohs reh-sep-TAH-koo-lohs eh-STEN koh-nek-TAH-thohs ah T'YEHR-rah)

Cut the wire.

Corte el alambre.
(KOR-teh el ah-LAHM-breh)

Remove the insulation from the wires.

Quite el aislamiento de los alambres.
(KEE-teh el ice-lahm-YEN-toh deh lohs ah-LAHM-bress)

Fasten the wall plates.

Asegure las placas de las paredes.
(ah-seh-GOO-reh lahs PLAH-kahs
deh lahs pah-REH-thess)

Secure the fixtures.

Asegure los ornamentos.
(ah-seh-GOO-reh lohs or-nah-
MEN-tohs)

Install the boxes 12 inches from the floor.

Instale las cajas a doce pulgadas del piso.
(een-STAH-leh lahs KAH-hahs ah
DOH-seh pool-GAH-thahs del
PEE-soh)

Place the ceiling fixture in the center of the room.

Ponga el ornamento del techo en el centro del cuarto.
(POHNG-gah el or-nah-MEN-toh del
TEH-choh en el SEN-troh del
KWAHR-toh)

Space the fixtures 4 feet apart.

Ponga los ornamentos cada cuatro pies.
(POHNG-gah lohs or-nah-MEN-tohs
kah-thah KWAH-troh-P'YESS)

Run the cable under the floor.

Corra el cable por debajo del piso.
(KOR-rah el KAH-bleh por deh-bah-
hoh del PEE-soh)

around the door

alrededor de la puerta
(ahl-reh-theh-THOR deh lah
PWEHR-tah)

Tools and Equipment

Use <u>pliers</u>.

Use <u>alicates</u>.
(OO-seh ah-lee-KAH-tess)

long-nose pliers

alicates de punta larga
(ah-lee-KAH-tess deh POON-
tah LAHR-gah)

lineman's pliers

alicates para cortar cables
(ah-lee-KAH-tess pah-rah
kor-TAHR KAH-bless)

a diagonal cutter

una cortadora de diagonales
(oo-nah kor-tah-THOR-ah deh
d'yah-goh-NAH-less)

wire strippers

un pelador de cable
(oon peh-lah-THOR deh KAH-
bleh)

a (Phillips head) screwdriver

**un destornillador (punta
de cruz)**
(oon dess-tor-nee-yah-THOR
[poon-tah deh CROOSE])

an insulated screwdriver

un destornillador aislado
(oon dess-tor-nee-yah-THOR
ice-LAH-thoh)

a conduit bender

un doblador de conduit
(oon doh-blah-THOR deh
kohn-D'WEET)

crimp connectors

**conectores de alambres
aplastados**
(koh-nek-TOR-ess deh
ah-LAHM-bress ah-plah-
STAH-thohs)

wire nuts	**conectores de cables** (koh-nek-TOR-ess deh KAH-bless)
electrical tape	**cinta eléctrica** (SEEN-tah eh-LEK-tree-kah)
a circuit tester	**un probador de circuitos** (oon proh-bah-THOR deh seer-KWEE-tohs)
a digital multimeter	**un multímetro digital** (oon mool-TEE-meh-troh dee-hee-TAHL)
a metal conduit	**un conduit de metal** (oon kohn-D'WEET deh meh-TAHL)
a PVC conduit	**un conduit de PVC** (oon kohn-D'WEET deh PEH-BEH-SEH)
NM-B cable	**cable interior / cable NM-B** (KAH-bleh een-teh-R'YOR) / (KAH-bleh EH-neh-EH-meh-BEH)
UF cable	**cable exterior / cable UF** (KAH-bleh eks-teh-R'YOR) / (KAH-bleh OO-EH-feh)
a utility knife	**una cuchilla para uso general** (oo-nah koo-CHEE-yah pah-rah OO-soh geh-neh-RAHL)
fish tape	**cinta pescadora** (SEEN-tah peh-skah-THOR-ah)

Heating and Air-Conditioning

In this section you will find phrases that refer to both heating and air-conditioning appliances and their installation. The words for *heating* and *air-conditioning* are:

heating	**la calefacción**
	(lah kah-lee-fahk-S'YOHN)
air-conditioning	**el aire acondicionado**
	(el EYE-reh ah-kohn-dee-s'yoh-
	NAH-thoh)

Elements of Heating and Air-Conditioning Systems

the furnace	**el calentador**
	(el kah-len-tah-THOR)
the boiler	**el calentador de agua**
	(el kah-len-tah-THOR de AH-gwah)
the motor	**el motor**
	(el moh-TOR)
the pump	**la bomba**
	(lah BOHM-bah)
the pipes	**los tubos**
	(lohs TOO-bohs)
the expansion tank	**el tanque de expansión**
	(el TAHNG-keh deh ek-spahn-S'YOHN)
the thermocouple	**el termopar**
	(el tehr-moh-PAHR)
the burners	**los quemadores**
	(lohs keh-mah-THOR-ess)
the pilot light	**el piloto**
	(el pee-LOH-toh)

the heat exchanger	**el repartidor de calefacción**
	(el reh-pahr-tee-THOR deh kah-leh-fahk-S'YOHN)
the blower	**el ventilador**
	(el ben-tee-lah-THOR)
the air return ducts	**los conductos del retorno del aire**
	(lohs kohn-DOOK-tohs del reh-TOR-noh del EYE-reh)
the delivery / supply duct	**el repartidor de aire**
	(el reh-pahr-tee-THOR deh EYE-reh)
the registers	**las aberturas de aire**
	(lahs ah-behr-TOO-rahs deh EYE-reh)
the radiator	**el radiador**
	(el rah-d'yah-THOR)
the baseboards	**los zócalos**
	(lohs SOH-kah-lohs)
the chimney	**la chimenea**
	(lah chee-meh-NEH-ah)
the thermostat	**el termostato**
	(el tehr-moh-STAH-toh)
central air-conditioning	**aire acondicionado central**
	(eye-reh ah-kohn-dee-s'yoh-NAH-thoh sen-TRAHL)
a window unit	**una unidad de ventana**
	(oo-nah oo-nee-THAD deh ben-TAH-nah)
a wall unit	**una unidad de pared**
	(oo-nah oo-nee-THAD deh pah-RED)
the condenser	**el condensador**
	(el kohn-den-sah-THOR)

the compressor	**el compresor**
	(el kohm-preh-SOR)
the fan	**el ventilador**
	(el ben-tee-lah-THOR)
the service panel	**el panel de servicio**
	(el pah-NELL deh sehr-BEE-s'yoh)
the refrigerant lines	**las líneas refrigerantes**
	(lahs LEE-neh-ahs reh-free-heh-
	RAHN-tess)
the drain line	**la línea de desagüe**
	(lah LEE-neh-ah deh dess-AH-gweh)
the filter	**el filtro**
	(el FEEL-troh)
the evaporator coil	**el evaporador de serpentina**
	(el eh-bah-poh-rah-THOR deh
	sehr-pen-TEE-nah)
the plenum	**el pleno**
	(el PLEH-noh)

Flooring

In this section you will find expressions for installing various types of flooring. You can find vocabulary for installing tiled floors under the heading "Tile Work" on page 122.

There are two common words for *floor* in Spanish.

floor	**el suelo**
	(el SWEH-loh)
	el piso
	(el PEE-soh)

Types of Flooring and Floor Covering

Here are the Spanish words for different types of finished flooring.

the subfloor	**el subpiso**
	(el soob-PEE-soh)
a <u>wood</u> floor	**un piso de madera**
	(oon pee-soh deh mah-THEH-rah)
hardwood	**de madera dura**
	(deh mah-theh-rah DOO-rah)
parquet	**de parqué**
	(deh pahr-KEH)
laminate	**de laminado**
	(deh lah-mee-NAH-thoh)
unfinished	**sin terminar**
	(seen tehr-mee-NAHR)
tongue-and-groove	**machihembrado**
	(mah-chee-em-BRAH-thoh)
prefinished	**pre-terminado**
	(preh-tehr-mee-NAH-thoh)
sheet vinyl	**de lámina de vinil**
	(deh LAH-mee-nah deh bee-NEEL)
wall-to-wall carpet	**de lámina de alfombra**
	(deh LAH-mee-nah deh ahl-FOHM-brah)
tiled	**de losas**
	(deh deh LOH-sahs)
vinyl	**de vinil**
	(deh bee-NEEL)
rubber	**de hule**
	(deh OO-leh)

linoleum	**de linóleo**
	(deh lee-NOH-leh-oh)
quarry	**de cantera**
	(deh kahn-TEH-rah)

Basic Tasks for Floor Installation

Level the floor.
> **Nivele el piso.**
> (nee-BEH-leh el PEE-soh)

Measure the surface area.
> **Mida el área.**
> (MEE-thah el AH-reh-ah)

Lay out the pattern.
> **Haga el plano.**
> (AH-gah el PLAH-noh)

Check the alignment frequently.
> **Cheque la alineación con frecuencia.**
> (CHEH-keh lah ah-lee-neh-ah-S'YOHN kohn freh-KWEN-s'yah)

Installing Wood Floors

Measure the flooring strips.
> **Mida las tiras.**
> (MEE-thah lahs TEE-rahs)

Cut the strips.
> **Corte las tiras.**
> (KOR-teh lahs TEE-rahs)

Draw a guideline on the floor.
> **Dibuje una línea de guía en el piso.**
> (dee-BOO-heh oo-nah LEEN-eh-ah deh GHEE-ah en el PEE-soh)

Notch the strips to fit around the doorjamb.
> **Haga cortes en las tiras para que quepan alrededor del quicio.**
> (AH-gah KOR-tess en lahs TEE-rahs pah-rah keh KEH-pahn ahl-reh-theh-THOR del KEESE-yoh)

Spread the adhesive on the subfloor.	**Unte el pegamento en el subpiso.**
	(OON-teh el peh-gah-MEN-toh en el soob-PEE-soh)
Fasten the flooring to the subfloor.	**Pegue el revestimiento al subpiso.**
	(PEH-geh el reh-bess-teem-YEN-toh ahl soob-PEE-soh)
Tap the strips with a block and hammer.	**Sujete las tiras con un bloque y un martillo.**
	(soo-HEH-teh lahs TEE-rahs kohn oon BLOH-keh ee oon mahr-TEE-yoh)
Nail the baseboards to the wall.	**Clave los zócalos a la pared.**
	(KLAH-beh lohs SOH-kah-lohs ah lah pah-RED)
Nail the molding to the baseboard.	**Clave las molduras al zócalo.**
	(KLAH-beh lahs mohl-DOO-rahs ahl SOH-kah-loh)
Trim the doorjamb.	**Recorte el quicio.**
	(reh-KOR-teh el KEESE-yoh)
Make sure the doorjamb is flush with the floor.	**Asegúrese que el quicio esté al nivel del piso.**
	(ah-seh-GOO-reh-seh keh el KEESE-yoh eh-STEH ahl nee-BELL del PEE-soh)
Sand the floor.	**Lije el piso.**
	(LEE-heh el PEE-soh)
Finish the floor.	**Termine el piso.**
	(tehr-MEE-neh el PEE-soh)
Apply three coats of varnish.	**Aplique tres capas de barniz.**
	(ah-PLEE-keh TRESS KAH-pahs deh bahr-NEESE)

Installing Sheet Flooring

Make sure the floor is dry.

Cheque que el piso esté seco.

(CHEH-keh keh el PEE-soh eh-STEH
   SEH-koh)

Install a vapor barrier.

Instale una barrera de vapor.

(een-STAH-leh oo-nah bahr-REH-rah
   deh bah-POR)

Fit the end of the roll against the
   long wall.

**Coloque el borde del rollo contra
   la pared más larga.**

(koh-LOH-keh el BOR-deh del ROH-
   yoh kohn-trah lah pah-RED MAHS
   LAHR-gah)

Make sure the pattern is parallel
   to the wall.

**Cheque que el diseño esté paralelo
   a la pared.**

(CHEH-keh keh el dee-SEN-yoh eh-
   STEH pah-rah-LEH-lo ah lah
   pah-RED)

Cut the sheet.

Corte la lámina.

(KOR-teh lah LAH-mee-nah)

Slide the edge up against the wall.

Ponga el borde contra la pared.

(POHNG-gah el BOR-deh kohn-trah
   lah pah-RED)

Flatten the sheet.

Aplane la lámina.

(ah-PLAH-neh lah LAH-mee-nah)

Notch the corners.

**Haga cortes pequeños en las
   esquinas.**

(AH-gah KOR-tess peh-KEN-yohs
   en lahs eh-SKEE-nahs)

Make notches to fit around the curves.	**Haga cortes para que quepa alrededor de las curvas.** (AH-gah KOR-tess pah-rah keh KEH-pah ahl-reh-theh-THOR deh lahs KOOR-bahs)
Overlap the second roll over the first one.	**Traspase el segundo rollo sobre el primero.** (trahs-PAH-seh el seh-GOON-doh ROH-yoh soh-breh el pree-MEH-roh)
Align the pattern.	**Alinee el diseño.** (ah-lee-NEH-eh el dee-SEN-yoh)
Cut through both surfaces.	**Corte las dos superficies.** (KOR-teh lahs DOHS soo-pehr-FEESE-yess)
Remove the waste strips.	**Quite los desperdicios.** (KEE-teh lohs dess-pehr-THEE-s'yohs)
Push all the edges in between the baseboard and the floor.	**Empuje los bordes entre el zócalo y el piso.** (em-POO-heh lohs BOR-dess en-treh el SOH-kah-loh ee el PEE-soh)
Trim it with a sharp knife.	**Recórtelo con una navaja bien afilada.** (reh-KOR-teh-loh kohn oo-nah nah-BAH-hah B'YEN ah-fee-LAH-thah)
Lift up the edge.	**Levante el borde.** (leh-BAHN-teh el BOR-deh)
Apply adhesive to the edge.	**Aplique pegamento al borde.** (ah-PLEE-keh peh-gah-MEN-toh ahl BOR-deh)

Installing Carpet

Spread out the carpet pad.

Despliegue el fieltro.

(dess-PL'YEH-geh el F'YELL-troh)

Install tack strips on the floor along the walls.

Instale las tiras de tachuelas en el piso a lo largo de las paredes.

(een-STAH-leh lahs TEE-rahs de tah-CH'WEH-lahs en el PEE-soh ah loh LAHR-goh deh lahs pah-REH-thess)

Roll out the carpet.

Despliegue la alfombra.

(dess-PL'YEH-geh lah ahl-FOHM-brah)

Place the edge against the long wall.

Coloque el borde contra la pared más larga.

(koh-LOH-keh el BOR-deh kohn-trah lah pah-RED MAHS LAHR-gah)

Attach the edge to the tack strip.

Conecte el borde a la tira de tachuelas.

(koh-NEK-teh el BOR-deh ah lah TEE-rah deh tah-CH'WEH-lahs)

Check the pattern alignment.

Cheque que el diseño esté alineado.

(CHEH-keh keh el dee-SEN-yoh eh-STEH ah-lee-neh-AH-thoh)

Stretch the carpet to the opposite wall.

Estire la alfombra hasta la pared opuesta.

(eh-STEE-reh lah ahl-FOHM-brah ah-stah lah pah-RED oh-PWEH-stah)

Flatten the carpet to the floor.

Aplane la alfombra.

(ah-PLAH-neh lah ahl-FOHM-brah)

Roll the carpet from the center toward the edges.

Aplane la alfombra desde el centro hacia los bordes.

(ah-PLAH-neh lah ahl-FOHM-brah dez-deh el SEN-troh ah-s'yah lohs BOR-dess)

Notch the corners.

Haga cortes en las esquinas.

(AH-gah KOR-tess en lahs eh-SKEE-nahs)

Press the carpet in between the baseboard and the floor.

Apriete la alfombra entre el zócalo y el piso.

(ah-PR'YEH-teh lah ahl-FOHM-brah en-treh el SOH-kah-loh ee el PEE-soh)

Trim it with a sharp knife.

Recórtela con una navaja bien afilada.

(re-KOR-teh-lah kohn oo-nah nah-BAH-hah B'YEN ah-fee-LAH-thah)

Nail the carpet to the subfloor.

Clave la alfombra al subpiso.

(KLAH-beh lah ahl-FOHM-brah ahl soob-PEE-soh)

Butt the second roll against the edge of the first.

Junte el segundo rollo al borde del primero.

(HOON-teh el seh-GOON-doh ROH-yoh ahl BOR-deh del pree-MEH-roh)

Attach the seam edges with adhesive.

Pegue los bordes con pegamento.

(PEH-geh lohs BOR-dess kohn peh-gah-MEN-toh)

Flooring Tools and Supplies

Use a pattern template.	**Use un patrón.**
	(OO-seh oon pah-TROHN)
a chalkline	**una línea de marcar**
	(oo-nah LEEN-eh-ah deh mahr-KAHR)
a contour gauge	**un indicador de contornos**
	(oon een-dee-kah-THOR deh kohn-TOR-nohs)
a coping saw	**una sierra de marquetería**
	(oo-nah S'YEHR-rah deh mahr-keh-teh-REE-ah)
a jigsaw	**una sierra de puñal**
	(oo-nah S'YEHR-rah deh poon-YAHL)
a circular saw	**una sierra circular**
	(oo-nah S'YEHR-rah seer-koo-LAHR)
a miter saw	**una sierra de retroceso**
	(oo-nah S'YEHR-rah deh reh-troh-SEH-soh)
a drill	**un taladro**
	(oon tah-LAH-droh)
a chisel	**un cincel**
	(oon seen-SELL)
a sharp knife	**una navaja bien afilada**
	(oo-nah nah-BAH-hah B'YEN ah-fee-LAH-thah)
a hammer	**un martillo**
	(oon mahr-TEE-yoh)

a small finish hammer	**un martillo suave**
	(oon mahr-TEE-yoh SWAH-beh)
a mallet	**un mazo**
	(oon MAH-soh)
a flooring nailer	**un clavador para pisos**
	(oon klah-bah-THOR pah-rah PEE-sohs)
nails	**clavos**
	(KLAH-bohs)
a notched trowel	**una paleta con muescas**
	(oo-nah pah-LEH-tah kohn MWEH-skahs)
a putty knife	**una espátula**
	(oo-nah eh-SPAH-too-lah)
a carpet stretcher	**un estirador de alfombras**
	(oon eh-stee-rah-THOR deh ahl-FOHM-brahs)
a flooring roller	**una aplanadora**
	(oo-nah ah-plah-nah-THOR-ah)
resin (rosin) paper	**papel de resina**
	(pah-PELL deh reh-SEE-nah)
a sander	**una lijadora**
	(oo-nah lee-hah-THOR-ah)
a drum sander	**una lijadora de bidón**
	(oo-nah lee-hah-THOR-ah de bee-THOHN)
an orbital sander	**una lijadora de órbito**
	(oo-nah lee-hah-THOR-ah deh OR-bee-toh)
a buffer	**una gamuza**
	(oo-nah gah-MOO-sah)

a vacuum cleaner

una aspiradora
(oo-nah ah-spee-rah-THOR-ah)

Painting

In this section you will find terms and expressions used in painting. In Spanish the word for *paint* is the same as the word for a *painting* that you could hang on a wall:

paint

la pintura
(lah peen-TOO-rah)

Safety

The following phrases will help you maintain the safety of your painters.

Make sure the ladder is sturdy.

Cheque que la escalera esté firme.
(CHEH-keh keh lah eh-skah-LEH-rah
eh-STEH FEER-meh)

scaffolding

el andamio
(el ahn-DAHM-yoh)

Be careful on the ladder.

**Tenga cuidado cuando esté en
la escalera.**
(TENG-gah kwee-THAH-thoh
kwahn-doh eh-STEH en lah
eh-skah-LEH-rah)

extension ladder

la escalera eregida
(lah eh-skah-LEH-rah
eh-reh-HEE-thah)

Keep both feet on the ladder.	**Mantenga los dos pies en la escalera.**
	(mahn-TENG-gah lohs DOHS P'YESS en lah eh-skah-LEH-rah)
Do not reach beyond arm's length.	**No se extienda más que su brazo.**
	(NOH seh eks-T'YEN-dah MAHS keh soo BRAH-soh)
Wear a <u>dust mask</u>.	**Lleve una <u>máscara</u>.**
	(YEH-beh oo-nah MAH-skah-rah)
goggles	**lentes de seguridad**
	(LEN-tess deh seh-goo-ree-THAD)

Painting Jobs

The following are some of the areas or things that you might ask your employees to paint.

Please paint . . .	**Por favor pinte...**
	(por fah-BOR PEEN-teh)
the exterior trim.	**las molduras del exterior.**
	(lahs mohl-DOO-rahs del eks-tehr-YOR)
the wood siding.	**el revestimiento de madera.**
	(el reh-behss-teem-YEN-toh deh mah-THEH-rah)
the deck.	**el 'deck'.**
	(el DEK)
the fence.	**la cerca.**
	(lah SEHR-kah)

the interior walls.	**las paredes del interior.**
	(lahs pah-REH-thess del een-tehr-YOR)
the ceilings.	**los techos.**
	(lohs TEH-chohs)
the baseboards.	**los zócalos.**
	(lohs SOH-kah-lohs)
the window frames.	**los marcos de las ventanas.**
	(lohs MAHR-kohs deh lahs ben-TAH-nahs)
the door frames.	**los marcos de las puertas.**
	(lohs MAHR-kohs deh lahs PWEHR-tahs)
the cabinets.	**los gabinetes.**
	(lohs gah-bee-NEH-tess)

Preliminary Tasks

Here are phrases for explaining how you would like the painters to proceed with a job.

Pick up the paint at the paint store.	**Vaya a la tienda de pinturas para recoger la pintura.**
	(BAH-yah ah lah T'YEN-thah deh peen-TOO-rahs pah-rah reh-koh-HEHR lah peen-TOO-rah)
Make sure the paint is the correct color.	**Cheque que el color de la pintura sea correcto.**
	(CHEH-keh keh el koh-LOR deh lah peen-TOO-rah seh-ah kor-REK-toh)

texture	**la textura**
	(lah teks-TOO-rah)
finish	**el acabado**
	(el ah-kah-BAH-thoh)
type	**el tipo**
	(el TEE-poh)
Cover the area with plastic sheeting.	**Ponga una cubierta de plástico.**
	(POHNG-gah oo-nah koob-YEHR-tah deh PLAH-stee-koh)
a drop cloth	**una lona**
	(oo-nah LOH-nah)
Scrape off the old paint.	**Quite la pintura original.**
	(KEE-teh lah peen-TOO-rah oh-ree-hee-NAHL)
Sand the area.	**Lije el área.**
	(LEE-heh el AH-reh-ah)
Put masking tape around . . .	**Ponga cinta adhesiva protectora en...**
	(POHNG-gah SEEN-tah ah-theh-SEE-bah proh-tek-TOR-ah en)
the adjoining areas of a different color.	**las áreas adyacentes de otro color.**
	(lahs AH-reh-ahs ahd-yah-SEN-tess deh oh-troh koh-LOR)
material	**material**
	(mah-tehr-YAHL)
Remove all the hardware.	**Quite toda la ferretería.**
	(KEE-teh TOH-thah lah fehr-reh-teh-REE-ah)

light fixtures	**las lámparas instaladas**
	(lahs LAHM-pah-rahs
	een-stah-LAH-thahs)
switch / outlet plates	**las placas de pared**
	(lahs PLAH-kahs deh pah-RED)
nails	**los clavos**
	(lohs KLAH-bohs)
picture hooks	**los ganchos para cuadros**
	(lohs GAHN-chohs pah-rah
	KWAH-drohs)
Patch the holes.	**Llene los agujeros.**
	(YEH-neh lohs ah-goo-HEH-rohs)
Sand the surface.	**Lije la superficie.**
	(LEE-heh lah soo-pehr-FEESE-yeh)
Make sure your brushes are clean.	**Cheque que las brochas estén limpias.**
	(CHEH-keh keh lahs BROH-chahs
	eh-STEN LEEMP-yahs)
Use a <u>new brush</u>.	**Use <u>una brocha nueva</u>.**
	(OO-seh oo-nah BROH-chah
	N'WEH-bah)
roller	**un rodillo (rollo) nuevo**
	(oon roh-THEE-yoh [ROH-yoh]
	N'WEH-boh)
Paint on a primer coat.	**Pinte una capa imprimadora.**
	(PEEN-teh oo-nah KAH-pah
	eem-pree-mah-THOR-ah)
Wait until the paint dries.	**Espere hasta que se seque la pintura.**
	(eh-SPEH-reh ah-stah keh seh
	SEH-keh lah peen-TOO-rah)

151

Put on the first coat.	**Pinte la primera capa.**
	(PEEN-teh lah pree-MEH-rah
	KAH-pah)
second	**segunda**
	(seh-GOON-dah)
Correct drips right away.	**Corrija las gotas en seguida.**
	(kor-REE-hah lahs GOH-tahs en
	seh-GHEE-thah)

Tools and Supplies for Painting Jobs

water-based paint	**pintura a base de agua**
	(peen-TOO-rah ah BAH-seh deh
	AH-gwah)
acrylic	**acrílica**
	(ah-KREE-lee-kah)
oil	**a base de aceite**
	(ah BAH-seh deh ah-SAY-teh)
flat	**mate**
	(MAH-teh)
semigloss	**semi-gloss**
	(seh-mee GLOHS)
high-gloss	**high-gloss**
	(HY-GLOHS)
satin-finish	**terminado de satín**
	(tehr-mee-NAH-thoh deh
	sah-TEENG)
eggshell	**terminado de cáscara**
	de huevo
	(tehr-mee-NAH-thoh deh KAHS-
	kah-rah deh WEH-boh)

Indoor Construction Work

paint thinner	**diluyente de pintura**
	(dee-loo-YEN-teh deh peen-TOO-rah)
paint remover	**removedor de pintura**
	(reh-moh-beh-THOR deh
	peen-TOO-rah)
turpentine	**la trementina**
	(lah treh-men-TEE-nah)
brush cleaner	**la limpiadora de brochas**
	(lah leemp-yah-THOR-ah deh
	BROH-chahs)
a <u>wide</u> brush	**una broche <u>ancha</u>**
	(oo-nah BROH-cheh AHN-chah)
narrow	**estrecha**
	(eh-STREH-chah)
touch-up	**de retoque**
	(deh reh-TOH-keh)
a power paint roller	**un rollo eléctrico**
	(oon ROH-yoh eh-LEK-tree-koh)
a roller tray	**una bandeja para el rollo**
	(oo-nah bahn-DEH-hah pah-rah
	el ROH-yoh)
a tray liner	**un cubridor de bandeja**
	(un koo-bree-THOR deh
	bahn-DEH-hah)
a power painting device	**una herramienta eléctrica**
	de pintura
	(oo-nah ehr-rahm-YEN-tah eh-LEK-
	tree-kah deh peen-TOO-rah)
a spray gun	**una pistola de pintura**
	(oo-nah pee-STOH-lah deh
	peen-TOO-rah)

a paint shield	**un protector de pintura**
	(oon proh-tek-TOR deh peen-TOO-rah)
masking tape	**la cinta adhesiva protectora**
	(lah SEEN-tah ah-theh-SEE-bah proh-tek-TOR-ah)
a bucket	**una cubeta**
	(oo-nah koo-BEH-tah)
a drop cloth	**una cubierta**
	(oo-nah koob-YEHR-tah)
a scraper	**un removedor**
	(oon reh-moh-beh-THOR)
a manual sander	**una lijadora manual**
	(oo-nah lee-hah-THOR-ah mahn-WAHL)
sandpaper	**el papel lija**
	(el pah-PELL LEE-hah)
the electric sander	**la lijadora eléctrica**
	(lah lee-hah-THOR-ah eh-LEK-tree-kah)

Cleaning Up

Clean up at the end of the day.	**Limpie al terminar el día.**
	(LEEMP-yeh ahl tehr-mee-NAHR el DEE-ah)
Clean your brushes.	**Limpie las brochas.**
	(LEEMP-yeh lahs BROH-chahs)

Indoor Construction Work

Keep a tight lid on the chemical products.

Tape bien los productos químicos.
(TAH-peh B'YEN lohs proh-THOOK-tohs KEE-mee-kohs)

When the paint is dry . . .

Cuando esté seca la pintura...
(kwahn-doh eh-STEH SEH-kah lah peen-TOO-rah)

check the area for mistakes

cheque que no haya errores.
(CHEH-keh keh noh ah-yah ehr-ROH-ress)

replace the hardware.

re-instale la ferretería.
(reh-een-STAH-leh lah fehr-reh-teh-REE-ah)

Make sure the windows open and close.

Cheque que las ventanas se abran y se cierren.
(CHEH-keh keh lahs ben-TAH-nahs seh AH-bran ee seh S'YEHR-ren)

doors

las puertas
(lahs PWEHR-tahs)

Take all your equipment with you.

Llévese todos sus aparatos.
(YEH-beh-seh TOH-thohs soos ah-pah-RAH-tohs)

Make sure the place is clean.

Cheque que el lugar esté limpio.
(CHEH-keh keh el loo-GAHR eh-STEH LEEMP-yoh)

Close and lock all the doors.

Cierre todas las puertas con llave.
(S'YEHR-reh TOH-thahs lahs PWEHR-tahs kohn YAH-beh)

Appendix

Numbers

0	**cero**	20	**veinte**
1	**uno**	21	**veintiuno**
2	**dos**	22	**veintidós**
3	**tres**	23	**veintitrés**
4	**cuatro**	24	**veinticuatro**
5	**cinco**	25	**veinticinco**
6	**seis**	26	**veintiséis**
7	**siete**	27	**veintisiete**
8	**ocho**	28	**veintiocho**
9	**nueve**	29	**veintinueve**
10	**diez**	30	**treinta**
11	**once**	31	**treinta y uno**
12	**doce**	32	**treinta y dos**
13	**trece**	33	**treinta y tres**
14	**catorce**	34	**treinta y cuatro**
15	**quince**	35	**treinta y cinco**
16	**dieciséis**	36	**treinta y seis**
17	**diecisiete**	37	**treinta y siete**
18	**dieciocho**	38	**treinta y ocho**
19	**diecinueve**	39	**treinta y nueve**

40	cuarenta	70	setenta
41	cuarenta y uno	71	setenta y uno
42	cuarenta y dos	72	setenta y dos
43	cuarenta y tres	73	setenta y tres
44	cuarenta y cuatro	74	setenta y cuatro
45	cuarenta y cinco	75	setenta y cinco
46	cuarenta y seis	76	setenta y seis
47	cuarenta y siete	77	setenta y siete
48	cuarenta y ocho	78	setenta y ocho
49	cuarenta y nueve	79	setenta y nueve
50	cincuenta	80	ochenta
51	cincuenta y uno	81	ochenta y uno
52	cincuenta y dos	82	ochenta y dos
53	cincuenta y tres	83	ochenta y tres
54	cincuenta y cuatro	84	ochenta y cuatro
55	cincuenta y cinco	85	ochenta y cinco
56	cincuenta y seis	86	ochenta y seis
57	cincuenta y siete	87	ochenta y siete
58	cincuenta y ocho	88	ochenta y ocho
59	cincuenta y nueve	89	ochenta y nueve
60	sesenta	90	noventa
61	sesenta y uno	91	noventa y uno
62	sesenta y dos	92	noventa y dos
63	sesenta y tres	93	noventa y tres
64	sesenta y cuatro	94	noventa y cuatro
65	sesenta y cinco	95	noventa y cinco
66	sesenta y seis	96	noventa y seis
67	sesenta y siete	97	noventa y siete
68	sesenta y ocho	98	noventa y ocho
69	sesenta y nueve	99	noventa y nueve

Appendix

100	cien	200	doscientos
101	ciento uno	300	trescientos
102	ciento dos	400	cuatrocientos
114	ciento catorce	500	quinientos
129	ciento veintinueve	600	seiscientos
133	ciento treinta y tres	700	setecientos
142	ciento cuarenta y dos	800	ochocientos
156	ciento cincuenta y seis	900	novecientos
167	ciento sesenta y siete	1000	mil
179	ciento setenta y nueve	2000	dos mil
188	ciento ochenta y ocho	2009	dos mil nueve
194	ciento noventa y cuatro	40,000	cuarenta mil
		1999	mil novecientos noventa y nueve
		1,000,000	un millón

English-Spanish Glossary

Expressions

Be careful.	Cuidado. / Tenga cuidado.
Call 9-1-1.	Llame al nueve-uno-uno.
Danger!	¡Peligro!
Don't . . .	No...
Excuse me.	Disculpe.
For how long . . . ?	¿Por cuánto tiempo...?
Good afternoon.	Buenas tardes.
Good evening.	Buenas tardes / noches.
Good morning.	Buenos días.
Good night.	Buenas noches.
Good-bye.	Adiós.
Hello.	Hola.
Help!	¡Auxilio!, ¡Socorro!
How . . . ?	¿Cómo...?, ¿Qué...?
How are you?	¿Cómo está usted?
How do you say . . . ?	¿Cómo se dice...?
How long have you lived here?	¿Hace cuánto que vive aquí?
How many . . . ?	¿Cuántos...?
How much . . . ?	¿Cuánto...?
I'm sorry.	Lo siento.
It depends.	Depende.
It's two o'clock.	Son las dos.
Maybe.	Quizás.
No.	No.
Please.	Por favor.
See you later.	Hasta luego.
Thank you.	Gracias.
Until when . . . ?	¿Hasta cuándo...?

Watch out for . . . !	¡Ojo con...!
Welcome.	Bienvenido-a-os-as.
What . . . ?	¿Cuál...?, ¿Qué...?
What day is today?	¿Qué día es hoy?
What for . . . ?	¿Para qué...?
What time is it?	¿Qué hora es?
What's your name?	¿Cuál es su nombre?
When . . . ?	¿Cuándo...?
Where . . . ?	¿Dónde...?
Where are you from?	¿De dónde es?
Where are you going?	¿Adónde va?
Where do you live?	¿Dónde vive?
Where is . . . ?	¿Dónde está...?
Who . . . ?	¿Quién...?
Who with . . . ?	¿Con quién...?
Whose is it?	¿De quién es?
Why . . . ?	¿Por qué?
Yes.	Sí.
You're welcome.	De nada.

People

anyone else	alguien más
boss	patrón/a, jefe/jefa
bricklayer	albañil
brother	hermano
carpenter	carpintero/a
coworker	colego/a, compañero/a
daughter	hija
ditchdigger	excavador/ora
doctor	doctor/ora, médico/a
driver	conductor/ora
electrician	electricista
father	papá
friend	amigo/a
gardener	jardinero/a
he	él
her	la, le
him	lo, le
husband	esposo
HVAC technician	técnico/a de calefacción y aire acondicionado
I	yo
installer	instalador/ora

laborer	obrero/a
landscaper	jardinero/a
mechanic	mecánico/a
mother	mamá
neighbor	vecino/a
operator	operador/ora
painter	pintor/ora
plumber	plomero/a
reference	referencia
refinisher	renovador/ora
roofer	constructor/ora de techos
she	ella
sister	hermana
son	hijo
supervisor	supervisor/ora
them	los, les
they	ellos/ellas
tile setter	experto/a en azulejos y losas
us	nos
we	nosotros/as
wife	esposa
worker	trabajador/ora, obrero/a, empleado/a
you	lo, la, le
you	usted
you all	ustedes

Words That Tell "Whose"

David's	de David
hers	suyo-a-os-as
his	suyo-a-os-as
mine	mío-a-os-as
ours	nuestro-a-os-as
the supervisor's	del supervisor/de la supervisora
theirs	suyo-a-os-as
yours	suyo-a-os-as

Places

area	área
attic	ático, desván
basement	sótano

bathroom	baño
bedroom	dormitorio, cuarto, recámara
city	ciudad
country (outskirts)	campo
danger zone	zona peligrosa
dining room	comedor
dump	tiradero
hall	pasillo
hardware store	ferretería
home, at	en casa
house	casa
kitchen	cocina
living room	sala
lumberyard	almacén de maderas
office	oficina, despacho
parking lot, in the	en el parqueo
place	lugar
porch	porche
restroom	baño, servicio
rock quarry	cantera
room	cuarto, habitación
shopping center	centro comercial
sidewalk	acera
site	sitio
suburbs	afueras
utility room	lavadero
worksite	sitio de trabajo

Words That Tell "Where"

across from	enfrente de
around	alrededor
at	en
back	para atrás
between	entre
downstairs	abajo
far away from	lejos de
forward	adelante
here	aquí
in back of	detrás de
in front of	delante de
inside	adentro
near	cerca de
next to	al lado de

on top of	encima de
outside	afuera
over there	allí
same place, in the	en el mismo lugar
there	ahí
under	debajo de
upstairs	arriba

Words That Tell "How"

carefully	con cuidado
clockwise	a la derecha
counterclockwise	a la izquierda
faster	más rápido
fine	bien
frequently	con frecuencia
horizontally	horizontalmente
like that	así
like this	así
not well	mal
on its side	de un lado
right side up	derecho
slowly	lento, despacio
so-so	regular / más o menos
upside down	al revés
vertically	verticalmente
well	bien

Words That Tell "When"

afterward	después, luego
always	siempre
at the end	al final
at three o'clock	a las tres
before	antes
early	temprano
every day	todos los días
first	primero
in advance	por adelantado
late	tarde
Monday, on	el lunes / los lunes
never	nunca

next week	la próxima semana
on time / punctual	puntual
same time, at the	al mismo tiempo
soon	pronto
the 5th of March	el cinco de marzo
today	hoy
tomorrow	mañana
until	hasta

Words That Tell "How Long"

a long time, for	un tiempo largo
a short time, for	un tiempo corto
a week, for	una semana
a year, for	un año
all day	todo el día
an hour, for	una hora
five minutes, for	cinco minutos

Words That Tell "How Much" or "How Many"

a few	unos/unas pocos-as
a little	un poco
a lot	mucho, muchos-as
extra	extra
few	pocos-as
one time	una vez
one-half	la mitad
several	varios-as
two times	dos veces

"Little Words"

against	contra
along	a lo largo de
apart	a una distancia de
because	porque
between	entre
if	si
in case of	en caso de
per	por

that (one)	ese, esa
these	estas, estos
those	esas, esos
through	por
to	a
toward	hacia
with (you, him, her, etc.)	con (usted, él, ella, etc.)
with me	conmigo
without	sin

Words That Describe People, Places, or Things

acoustic	acústico-a-os-as
acrylic	acrílico-a-os-as
adjustable	ajustable-s
bad	malo-a-os-as
black	negro-a-os-as
blue	azul-es
clean	limpio-a-os-as
coarse-thread	de rosca gruesa
completed	completado-a-os-as
correct	correcto-a-os-as
corrugated	corrugado-a-os-as
dry	seco-a-os-as
entire	entero-a-os-as
excess	de sobra
fine-thread	de rosca fina
fired	despedido-a-os-as
fire-rated	calificado-a-os-as para el fuego
fire-resistant	resistente-s al fuego
flat (paint)	mate
galvanized	galvanizado-a-os-as
good	bueno-a-os-as
green	verde-s
grounded	conectado-a-os-as a la tierra
heavy (thick)	grueso-a-os-as
heavy (weight)	pesado-a-os-as
horizontal	horizontales
hurt	herido-a-os-as
important	importante-s
installed	instalado-a-os-as
large	grande-s
level	nivel
load-bearing	de carga

loose	suelto-a-os-as
mixed	mezclado-a-os-as
motorized	motorizado-a-os-as
necessary	necesario-a-os-as
new	nuevo-a-os-as
oil-based	a base de aceite
orange	anaranjado-a-os-as
original, old	original-es
parallel	paralelo-a-os-as
plumb	a plomo
precise	preciso-a-os-as
preformed	preformado-a-os-as
protruding	que sobresalgan
red	rojo-a-os-as
rigid	rígido-a-os-as
rotted	podrido-a-os-as
satin-finish	terminado-a-os-as de satín
sharp	bien afilado-a-os-as, agudo-a-os-as
sick	enfermo-a-os-as
single	sencillo-a-os-as
small	pequeño-a-os-as
square	cuadrado-a-os-as
sturdy	firme-s
unfinished	no terminado-a-os-as
unskilled	sin especializaciones
urgent	urgente-s
warped	combado-a-os-as
water-based	a base de agua
water-resistant	resistente al agua
weather-resistant	resistente al agua y al viento
white	blanco-a-os-as
yellow	amarillo-a-os-as

Things

2 × 4	dos por cuatro
2 × 6	dos por seis
ABS	ABS
accident	accidente
acoustic tile	panel acústico
adapter	adaptador
address	dirección
adhesive	adhesiva
aggregate	conglomerado, agregado

air ducts	conductos de aire
air space	espacio de aire
air-conditioning	aire acondicionado
central	central
wall unit	unidad de pared
window unit	unidad de ventana
alignment	alineación
aluminum	aluminio
anchor	anclaje
anchor bolts	pernos de anclaje
apartment	apartamento, departamento
appliance	electrodoméstico, aparato
asphalt	asfalto
aviation snips	tijeras de aviación
backhoe	excavadora trasera
bale	bala
barrier	barrera
baseboard	zócalo
bathtub	bañera, tina
whirlpool	Jacuzzi
batt	pieza de tela
battery	batería
beam	viga
beeper	biper
bidet	bidé
block (substance)	bloque
blower	ventilador
board	plancha
body harness	arnés del cuerpo
boiler	calentador de agua
bolts	pernos
bottom plate	solera inferior
bracing	tirantes
break (rest)	descanso
breaker	interruptor automático
vacuum	interruptor de vacío
breaker panel	panel de interruptores automáticos
brick	ladrillo
bridge	puente
brush (for cleaning)	cepillo
brush (for painting)	brocha
bucket	cubeta
buffer	gamuza
building	edificio
bulldozer	niveladora

burner	quemador
burr	rebaba
bush	arbusto
cabinet	gabinete
cable	cable
caliper	calibrador
can	lata
can opener	abrelatas
carpet	alfombra
wall-to-wall	lámina de alfombra
carpet stretcher	estirador de alfombras
cash	efectivo
casing	moldura del marco de la ventana / puerta
caulking	goma para sellar, masilla
caulking gun	selladora, pistola de koking
ceiling	techo
ceiling box	caja del techo
ceiling fixture	ornamento del techo
cement	cemento
cement mixer	homigonera
center	centro
certification	certificación
chair rail	moldura para las sillas
chalk	tiza
chalkline	línea de marcar
check	cheque
chemical products	productos químicos
chimney	chimenea
chisel	cincel
circuit	circuito
individual	individual
circuit tester	probador de circuitos
clamp	abrazadera
claw hammer	martillo chivo
cleanout	registro
clearance	espacio
cloth	trapo
clutch	embrague
coat (layer)	capa, mano
code	código
color	color
column	columna
compactor	compactador
compressor	compresor

concrete	concreto
concrete board	tabla de concreto
condenser	condensador
conduit, metal	conduit de metal
conduit, PVC	conduit de PVC
cones	conos
connector, crimp	conector de alambre aplastado
construction	construcción
contour gauge	indicador de contornos
conveyor	transportador
copper	cobre
corner (inside)	rincón
corner (outside)	esquina
corner bead	protector de esquinas
course	curso
cover	cubierta
crack	grieta
crimp connector	conector de alambre aplastado
crowbar	palanca
crown molding	moldura para la cornisa
culvert	alcantarilla
curb	borde
curve	curva
day	día
debris	escombros
deck (outside)	deck
deck (subfloor)	losa de desplante
depth gauge	indicador de profundidad
design	diseño
diagonal cutter	cortadora de diagonales
diesel fuel	combustible diesel
digging bar	palanca excavadora
digital multimeter	multímetro digital
dimmer	regulador de luz
dirt	tierra
dishwasher	lavaplatos
ditch	zanja
document	documento
dollar	dólar
door	puerta
end	del extremo
exterior	exterior
folding	plegadiza
front	principal
garage	del garaje

interior	interior
panel	de paneles
pre-hung	pre-colgada
screen	de tela metálica
sliding	corrediza
storm	para tormentas
door knocker	aldaba, tocador
doorbell	timbre
doorjamb	quicio
doorknob	manilla
doorstop	tope
doorway	marco de la puerta, portal
drain	desagüe
floor	del piso
main	principal
storm	alcantarilla
drainpipe	sumidero, tubo de drenaje
drawer	cajón
drawing	dibujo
drips	gotas
driveway	entrada a la casa
drop cloth	cubierta de lona
drywall	muro en seco, tablón de yeso
drywall lifter	gato de muro en seco
drywall router	contorneadora para muro en seco
drywall saw	serrucho de punta
duct, air return	conductos del retorno del aire
duct, delivery / supply	repartidor de aire
duct tape	cinta de pega
dump truck	camión de carga, camión de volteo
dumpster	contenedor para escombros
dust mask	máscara contra el polvo
earplugs	tapones para los oídos
edge	borde
electrical box	caja eléctrica
electrical tape	cinta eléctrica
electricity	electricidad
emergency	emergencia
end (of a piece of material)	extremo
epoxy patch	resina epoxídica
equipment	aparatos, equipo
heavy	pesado
evaporator coil	evaporador de serpentina
exhaust fan	ventilador de extracción
expansion tank	tanque de expansión

experience	experiencia
face shield	máscara
fall arrester	sistema de detención de caídas
fan	ventilador
ceiling	del techo
exhaust	de extracción
faucet	llave del agua
feet	pies
felt	felpa
fence	cerca
fertilizer	fertilizante
fiberglass	fibra de vidrio
file	lima
filter	filtro
finish (of a surface)	acabado
fireplace	chimenea
first aid	primeros auxilios
fish tape	cinta pescadora
fitting	accesorio, conector
bushing	anillo de reducción
cap	tapa
coupling	cople
elbow	codo
plug	de rosca
reducer	reductor
T	en T
Y	en Y
flashing	tapajuntas
flashlight	linterna
floodlight	reflector de haz difuso
floor	piso, suelo
hardwood	de madera dura
laminate	de laminado
linoleum-tiled	de losas de linóleo
parquet	de parqué
prefinished	pre-terminado
sheet vinyl	de lámina de vinil
tiled	de losas
tongue-and-groove	machihembrado
unfinished	sin terminar
flooring strips	tiras
flux	fundete
footing	zarpa
forklift	montacargas
forms	encofrados

English-Spanish Glossary

foundation	cimiento
framing	armadura, marco
front-end loader	cargador delantero
fuel	combustible
furnace	calentador
gap	espacio
garage	garaje
garbage disposer	triturador
gas (for vehicle)	gasolina
gas (heating)	gas
gas line	línea de gas
gauge	indicador
generator, backup	generador de emergencia
girder	viga principal
gloves	guantes
glue	pegamento, goma
goggles	lentes de seguridad
gravel	grava
grid	sistema de rejas
grout	lechada
grout float	flota de calidad
guide (for door)	guía
guideline	línea de guía
gutter	canal
hacksaw	sierra/ serrucho
hammer	martillo
claw	chivo
framing	para marcos
shingling	para tablas
small finish	suave
hammer tacker	grapadora martillo
hanger	gancho
pipe	para tubos
hanger bracket	ménsula
hard hat	casco
header	cabezal
heat exchanger	repartidor de calefacción
heater, hot-water	calentador del agua
heating	calefacción
heavy equipment	equipo pesado
highway	autopista
hinge	bisagra
hoe	azadón
hold-down	pieza de anclaje
hole (in ground)	hoyo

hole (small)	agujero
hook	gancho
hose	manguera
hot-water heater	calentador del agua
hour	hora
house wrap	envoltura de material resistente al agua y al viento
housing	caja
HVAC	calefacción, ventilación y aire acondicionado
inch	pulgada
income	ingresos
instructions	instrucciones
insulation	aislamiento
jack (lifter)	gato
ladder	de escalera
pump	de andamio
jack (trimmer)	montante para sostener el cabezal
jigsaw	sierra de puñal
job	trabajo
joint	junta
joint compound	masilla, compuesto de juntas, pasta
joint tape	cinta para juntas
joist	viga, vigueta
joist hangers	estribos para viguetas
jumper cables	cables de arranque
key	llave
knee pads	protector de rodillas
knife	navaja
utility	cuchilla para uso general
ladder	escalera
extension	eregida
ladder jack	gato de escalera
law	ley
layout	trazo
lead	plomo
leak (fuel)	fuga (de combustible)
leak (pipe)	gotera
lid	tapa
light fixture	lámpara, luz
flourescent	fluorescente
outdoor	de afuera
recessed	recesada
track	de riel
light, flood	reflector de haz difuso

line	línea
drain	de desagüe
refrigerant	refrigerante
lockset	cerradura
lot	parcela
machine	máquina
mallet	mazo
manhole	registro
masking tape	cinta adhesiva protectora
masonry material	material de albañilería
material (substance)	material
mattock	zapapico
measurements	medidas
metal	metal
mildew	moho
mistakes	errores
miter box	caja de ángulos
miter saw	sierra de retroceso para ingletes
molding	moldura, molding
money	dinero
mortar	mezcla
motor	motor
nail pouch	bolsa para los clavos
nailer, flooring	clavador para pisos
nailgun	clavadora
notcher	entallador
nuts	tuercas
oil	aceite
opening	abertura
outlet, 240-volt	enchufe de 240 voltios
outlet plates	placas de pared
paint	pintura
paint remover	removedor de pintura
paint shield	protector de pintura
paint thinner	diluyente de pintura
pane	vidrio marcado
panel	panel
part	parte
partition	partición
pattern template	patrón
paver	losa
pick	pico
pickup truck	camioneta
picture hooks	ganchos para cuadros
picture rail	moldura para los cuadros

piece	pedazo
pile	pila
pilot light	piloto
pipe-joint compound	compuesto para tubos
pipes	tubos
plan (drawing)	plano
plank	tablón
plenum	pleno
pliers	alicates
lineman's	para cortar cables
long-nose	de punta larga
plumb bob	plomo
plumb line	plomada
plumbing	plomería
plunger	sopapa
post	poste
posthole digger	poseras
potholes	hoyos
power auger	barrena
power painting device	herramienta eléctrica de pintura
pressure	presión
primer (paint)	capa imprimadora
problem	problema
product	producto
project	proyecto
propane	propano
protective equipment	protección personal
pump	bomba
pump jack	gato de andamio
putty	masilla
putty knife	espátula
PVC	PVC
radiator	radiador
rafters	cabrios
rag	trapo
railing	pasamanos
range finder	telémetro
rasp	rectificadora de mano
rebar	varilla de refuerzo
receptacle	enchufe
GFI	GFI
refrigerant lines	líneas refrigerantes
refrigerator	nevera, refrigerador
register	abertura de aire, escape, registro
regulations	reglamentos

resin / rosin paper	papel de resina
respirator	máscara respiradora
ripout tool	herramienta de arrancar
road	camino, carretera
roadbed	la base para la carretera
rock	piedra
rock crusher	trituradora
roll (of carpet, sheeting)	rollo
roller (paint)	rodillo, rollo
roller (wheel)	ruedita
roller, flooring	aplanadora
roller, power paint	rollo eléctrico
roof	techo
roofing nailer	clavadora para techos
root	raíz
router	contorneadora
row (line)	fila
rubber	de goma
rubbing stone	piedra pómez
ruler	regla
safety belt	cinturón de seguridad
safety harness	arnés de seguridad
sand	arena
sander	lijadora
drum	de bidón
manual	manual
orbital	órbito
sandpaper	papel lija
saw	sierra, serrucho
carbide hole	de carbudo
circular	circular
coping	de marquetería
drywall	de punta
for tiles	para azulejos
grout	para lechada
hack	serrucho
jig	de puñal
sawhorse	burro
scaffolding	andamio
scraper	removedor
screw	tornillo
screwdriver	desarmador / destornillador
electric	eléctrico
insulated	aislado
Phillips head	cruz
screwgun	pistola de tornillo

seam	juntura
section	sección
segment	segmento
septic system	sistema séptico
septic tank	pozo séptico
sewer	alcantarilla
sewer pipes	cañerías para la alcantarilla
sheathing	entablado
sheet (of material)	hoja
sheet (of vinyl)	lámina
sheeting	cubierta
shelf	repisa
shim	cuña
shingle	tabla, hoja, teja de asfalto
shingling hammer	martillo para tablas
shovel	pala
shower	ducha
shutoff valve	válvula de cierre
sidewalk	acera
siding	revestimiento, siding
sign	señal
sill cock	grifo de manguera
sill plate	solera inferior
silt	limo
sink, bathroom	lavabo
sink, kitchen	fregadero
skylight	claraboya
sledgehammer	marro
smoke alarm	alarma contra fuego
snake	serpiente
soil pipe	tubo de residuos cloacales
soil stack	bajante
solvent	solvente
spill	derrame
sponge	esponja
spray gun	pistola de pintura
spud	palanca excavadora
square	escuadra
staple	grapa
stapler	grapadora
steps	escaleras
stone	piedra
stopper	tapón
storm drain	alcantarilla
stove	estufa

English-Spanish Glossary

straw	paja
street	calle
strip	listón
structure	estructura
stucco	estuco
stud	montante
stump	tocón
subfloor	subpiso
suelo	ground, floor
sump pump	bomba del sumidero
supply, water	suministro de agua
surface	superficie
switch	interruptor
switch plates	placas de pared
single-pole	de una vía
three-way	de tres vías
tack strip	tira de tachuela
tape	cinta
adhesive	adhesiva
duct	cinta de pega
masking	adhesiva protectora
tape measure	cinta métrica
tar	brea
tar paper	papel de brea
tarp	lona
task	tarea
telephone number	número de teléfono
texture	textura
thermocouple	termopar
thermostat	termostato
thing	cosa
thread (on pipe)	rosca
threshold	umbral
tie	tirante
tile	panel
acoustic	panel acústico
floor	losa
roofing	tabla, teja
sidewalk	baldosa
wall	azulejo
tile nipper	pinza para cortar losetas
tin snips	tijeras para escaño
tire	llanta
toilet	inodoro
toilet flange	palanca del inodoro

tool	herramienta
toolbelt	cinturón de herramientas
toolbox	caja de herramientas
top plate	solera superior
torch	antorcha
towtruck	grúa
track	carril
tractor	tractor
traffic	tráfico
trailer (of a truck)	remolque
trailer (on site)	trailer
training	entrenamiento
trap	trampa
trash	basura
trash can	basurero
tray	bandeja
tray liner	cubridor de bandeja
trench	trinchera
trencher	trinchador
trim	molduras
exterior	del exterior
trowel	paleta
flat	plana
notched	con muescas
truck	camión
truss	cercha de madera
turpentine	trementina
twine	macate
type	tipo
vacuum cleaner	aspiradora
valence	bastidor
valve	válvula
antisiphon	de antisifón
ball	de bola
drain	para drenar
multiple control	de control múltiple
shutoff / stop	de cierre
single-control	de control sencillo
van	camioneta
vapor barrier	barrera de vapor
varnish	barniz
vent	escape
vent line	respiradero
vent pipes	escapes
vibrator, electric	compactador

vibrator, pneumatic	vibrador pneumático, bailarina
vinyl	vinil
vise	prensa, tornillo de banco
wall	pared
wall plates	placas de la pared
warehouse	almacén
washers	arandelas
washing machine	lavadora
waste	desperdicios
water	agua
week	semana
welder	soldador
welding rod	barra de soldar
wheelbarrow	carretilla
window	ventana
casement	con bisagras
double-hung	de doble vía
fixed	fija
picture	ventanal
pivot	de pivote
pre-hung	precolgada
screen	de tela metálica
storm	contraventana, de tormenta
wire	alambre, cable
wire nuts	conectores de cables
wire stripper	pelador de cable
wood	madera
wrench	llave
adjustable	inglesa
basin	pico de ganso
crescent	de tuercas
pipe	de tubo

Activities

Note: In this section, the words for activities are given in their "infinitive" form, one that does not indicate "who" is doing the action. In the text of the book, most of the "action words" are given in the command form, appropriate for giving instructions.

align	alinear
alternate	alternar

English-Spanish Glossary

anchor	sujetar
apply	aplicar
assemble	armar
attach	pegar
back up	venir para atrás
bag	poner en la bolsa
bend	doblar
block	bloquear
blow	soplar
brake	frenar
break, break up	romper
build up	aumentar
butt	juntar al borde de
buy	comprar
call	llamar
calm down	calmarse
can (be able to)	poder
caulk	enmasillar, kokear
cement	aplicar cemento
change	cambiar
check	checar
clean	limpiar
clear	sacar
close	cerrar
close tightly	tapar
come	venir
compress	comprimir
concentrate	concentrar
connect	conectar
contact	contactar
cope	rematar con albardilla
correct	corregir
cover	cubrir
cut	cortar
dig	excavar
direct	dirigir
disturb	estorbar
do	hacer
drain	drenar, vaciar
draw (a diagram)	dibujar
drill	taladrar
drive	manejar
dry	secar
erect	construir
expect	esperar
fasten	asegurar, pegar, sujetar

English-Spanish Glossary

fill, fill up	llenar
finish	terminar
fire	despedir
fit	caber
flare	abocinar
flatten	aplanar
flip (a switch)	prender
give	dar
go	ir
ground	poner tierra
happen	pasar
have	tener
help	ayudar
hire	contratar
hold	sostener
hurt	doler
install	instalar
join	juntar
keep	mantener
last	durar
lay	colocar
leave (go out)	salir
leave (something)	dejar
level	nivelar
lift, lift up	levantar
load	cargar
lock	cerrar con llave
look for	buscar
loosen	soltar
lower	bajar
make sure	checar, asegurarse
mark	marcar
measure	medir
miter	sesgar
mix	mezclar
move	mover
must	deber
nail	clavar
need	necesitar
open	abrir
overlap	traslapar
paint	pintar
patch	llenar
pave	pavimentar
pay	pagar

English-Spanish Glossary

pick up	recoger
place	colocar
pour	echar
press	apretar, presionar
pull	jalar
push	empujar
put	poner
put up	parar, montar
raise (make bigger)	aumentar
raise (make higher)	subir, levantar
rake	rastrillar
raze	arrasar
reach	extenderse
reinstall	reinstalar
remove	quitar
repair	reparar
replace	reemplazar
resurface	ponerle una superficie nueva
return, come back, go back	regresar, volver
run (a wire)	correr
sand	lijar
score	hacer cortes
scrape off	quitar
seal	pegar, masillar
secure	asegurar
separate	separar
signal	indicar
slope	hacer un desnivel
smooth	alisar
spray	salpicar
spread (a paste)	untar
spread out, unfold	desplegar
start	empezar
stay	quedarse
stop	parar
stretch	estirar
sweep	barrer
take, carry	llevar
take out (remove)	sacar
tear down	desmantelar
tell	decir
tighten	apretar
touch	tocar
trim	recortar
turn around	darse una vuelta

turn (something) around	darle la vuelta
turn (something) over	voltear
turn off (light, machine)	apagar (la luz, la máquina)
turn off (water)	cerrar (la llave del agua)
turn on (light, machine)	encender (la luz, la máquina)
turn on (water)	abrir (la llave del agua)
unclog	quitar la obstrucción
understand	entender, comprender
unload	descargar
use	usar
varnish	barnizar
wait	esperar
watch	mirar
wipe	pasar un trapo por
work	trabajar
write down	anotar
yell	gritar